SECOND GRADE SKIL
TABLE OF CONTENT

SECOND GRADE SKILLS

INTRODUCTION
This book is designed to reinforce basic second grade skills. Each lesson provides a foundation for learning more advanced skills taught in later grades and offers an enjoyable learning experience for the child.

ORGANIZATION
Each of the six sections contains a variety of activities that focus on basic skills.

- **PHONICS**: This section contains a variety of activities that reinforce basic skills essential for beginning readers: understanding short and long vowels, recognizing vowel and letter sounds in words, pronouncing vowel sounds, writing words, and reading.

- **CRITICAL THINKING**: These important skills of reading, thinking, and reasoning will help the child in all subject areas: following directions, comparing, outlining, classifying, identifying relationships, sequencing, and recognizing action words and naming words.

- **READING COMPREHENSION:** The reading samples allow the child to think creatively by titling stories to show understanding of main idea. The enjoyable activities and stories in this section minimize frustration for beginning readers.

- **CLOZE:** Practicing the CLOZE method will familiarize the child with this type of testing without pressure and frustration. Working with CLOZE exercises helps to expand students' vocabulary and increase critical thinking ability. After completing this section, students will have an increased understanding of word usage and meaning.

- **MATH:** This section reviews basic math skills taught in second grade, including understanding addition, subtraction, and problem-solving strategies and skills.

- **SCIENCE IDEAS:** These simple, enjoyable activities require a minimum of supplies to provide a fun, easy way for a child to experiment with science. Students will review classifying foods, separating mixtures, understanding Earth layers, and ordering events/seasons.

USE

This book is designed for independent use by students who have had instruction in the specific skills covered in the lessons. Copies of the activities can be given to individuals, pairs of students, or small groups for completion. They can also be used as a center activity. If students are familiar with the content, the worksheets can also be used as homework.

To begin, determine the implementation which fits your students' needs and your classroom structure. The following plan suggests a format for this implementation:

1. **Explain** the purpose of the worksheets to your class. Let students know that these activities will be fun as well as helpful.

2. **Review** the mechanics of how you want students to work with the activities. Do you want them to work in groups? Are these activities for homework?

3. **Introduce** students to the process and to the purpose of the activities. Go over the directions. Work with children when they have difficulty. Work only a few pages at a time to avoid pressure.

4. **Do** a practice activity together.

ADDITIONAL NOTES

1. **Parent Communication** Sign the *Letter to Parents* and send it home with students.

2. **Bulletin Board** Display completed activities to show student progress.

3. **Center Activities** Use the worksheets as center activities to give students the opportunity to work cooperatively.

4. **Assessment Test** Administer the Assessment Test before and after completion of the activities. This tool provides evidence of progress.

5. **Have fun** Working with these activities can be fun as well as meaningful for you and your students.

Name ______________________ Date ____________________

Assessment

 Circle the pictures that have **short vowel** sounds. Put an X on the pictures that have **long vowel** sounds.

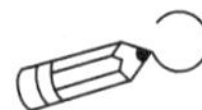 Write the letter of the picture that is different in each row.

a **b** **c** **d** ______

a **b** **c** **d** ______

Circle the naming part of each sentence in blue.

Circle the action part of each sentence in red.

1. My friend goes to the zoo with me.
2. Monkeys climb trees.
3. Tigers roar loudly.

Name ______________________ Date ____________________

Assessment

Write the number in the box.

1. 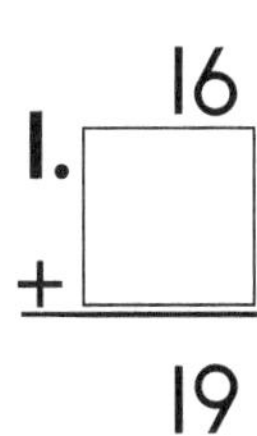

16
+ ☐
19

2.

☐
− 2
15

3.

13
− ☐
8

4.

9
+ ☐
16

---

5. Jodi's cat had 5 kittens. Sari's cat had 6 kittens. How many kittens did the girls have in all? 

---

6. Write the next number in the pattern. 2 → 4 → 7 → 11 → ___

7. Find 2 different ways to buy the cookie. Write how many of each coin you need.

---

8. Name four main food groups.

__________ __________ __________ __________

9. When you pour water and sand into a filter, what happens to the sand? ______________________________

10. Name the four seasons.

__________ __________ __________ __________

Dear Parent,

During this school year, our class will be working with activities in reading, writing, mathematics, and science. We will be completing activity sheets that provide practice to ensure mastery of these important skills.

From time to time, I may send home activity sheets. To best help your child, please consider the following suggestions:

- Provide a quiet place to work.
- Go over the directions together.
- Encourage your child to do his or her best.
- Check the lesson when it is complete.
- Go over your child's work, and note improvements as well as problems.

Help your child maintain a positive attitude about the activities. Let your child know that each lesson provides an opportunity to have fun and to learn. Above all, enjoy this time you spend with your child. He or she will feel your support, and skills will improve with each activity completed.

Thank you for your help!

Cordially,

Name ______________________ Date ____________________

Color the pictures with names that have the **short vowel** sound of the letter in the box.

Name ______________________ Date ____________________

Color the pictures with names that have the **long vowel** sound of the letter in the box.

o

 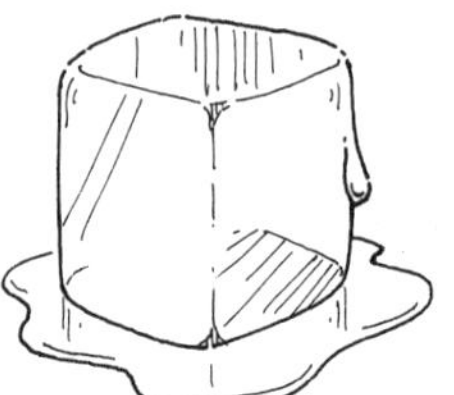 

a

u

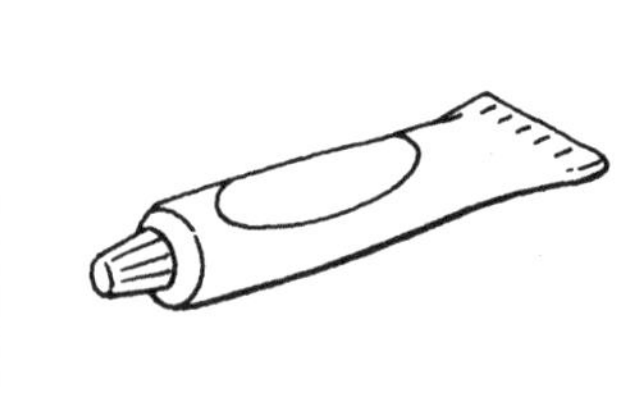 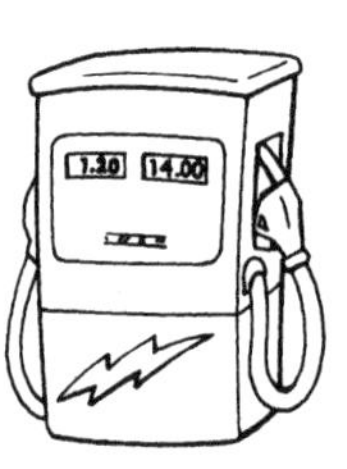 

 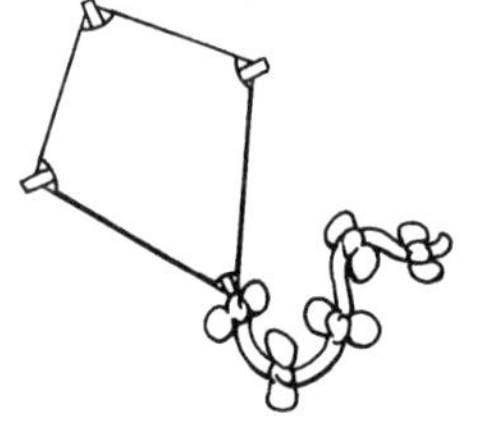 

Name ______________________ Date ____________________

Color the pictures with names that have the **long vowel** sound red. Color the pictures with names that have the **short vowel** sound green.

Name ______________________ Date ____________________

Circle the words that have the **short a** sound.
Put an X on the words that have the **long a** sound.

lake	hay
cap	rain
safe	bag
vase	lamp
pan	bat

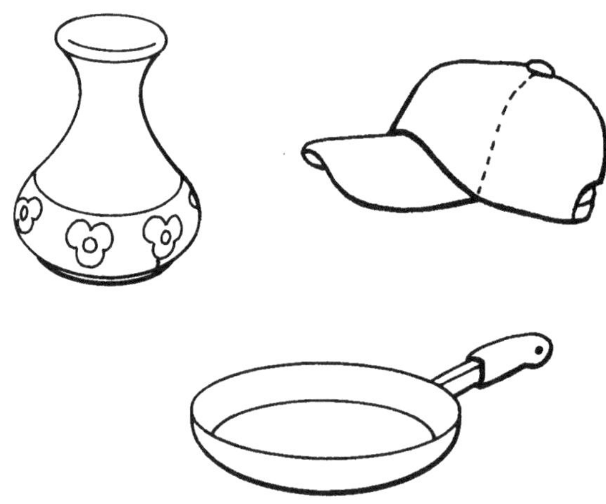

Draw a picture of a word from the box that has the **long a** sound. Write the name of the picture.

Draw a picture of a word from the box with the **short a** sound. Write the name of the picture.

Name ______________________ Date ________________

Write the name of the picture with **a_e** if you hear the long **a** sound.

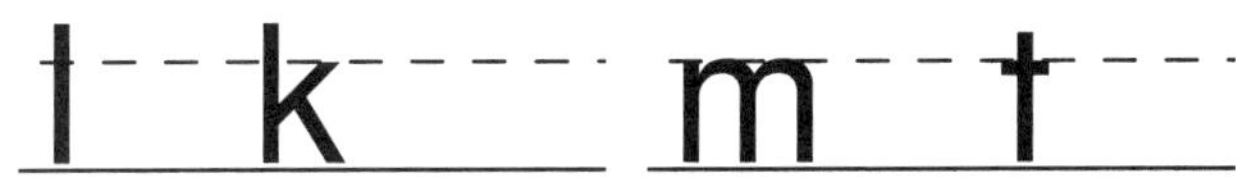

l k m t

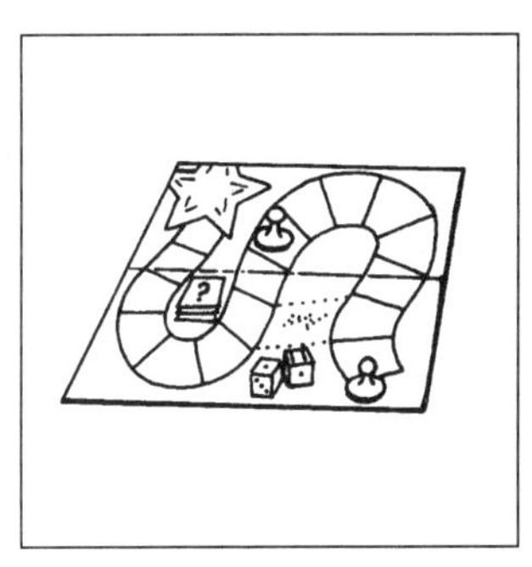

g m f n

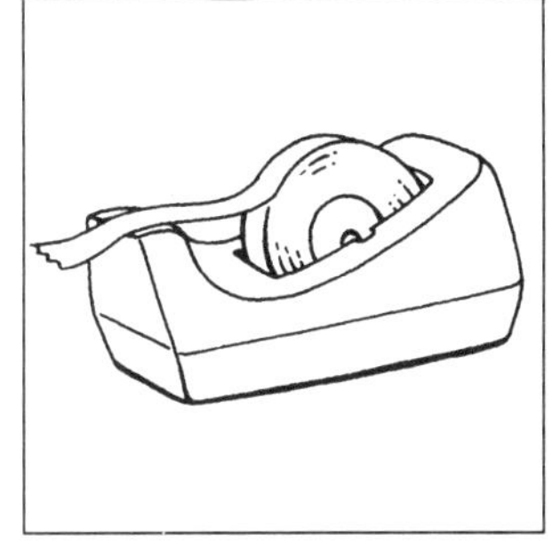

t p c k

The letters **ai** and **ay** can stand for the long **a** sound.

Circle the picture name.

Write the name.

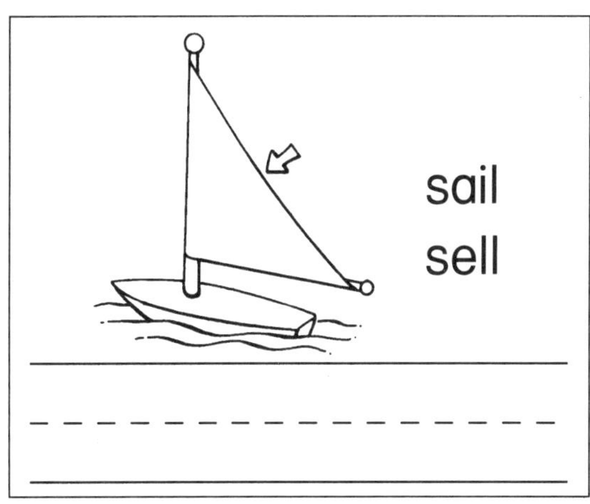

Name ______________________ Date ______________________

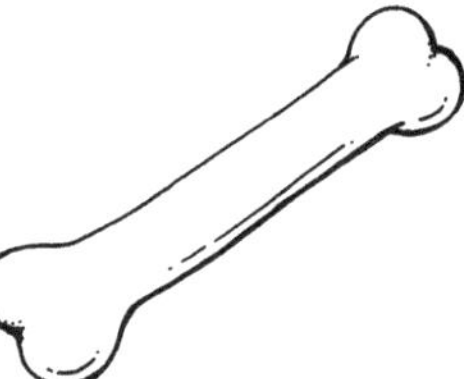

Circle the words that have the short **o** sound.
Put an X on the words that have the long **o** sound.

note	fox	nose	home	log
rope	rock	rose	sock	mop

Draw a picture of a word from the box that has the long **o** sound. Write the name of the picture.

____

Draw a picture of a word from the box with the short **o** sound. Write the name of the picture.

____

Short and Long o

Name ______________________ Date ____________________

Write the name of the picture with **o_e** if you hear the long **o** sound.

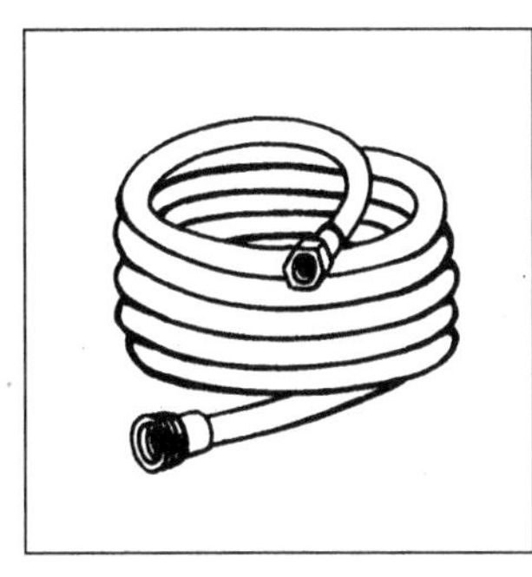

h __ s __ c __ n __

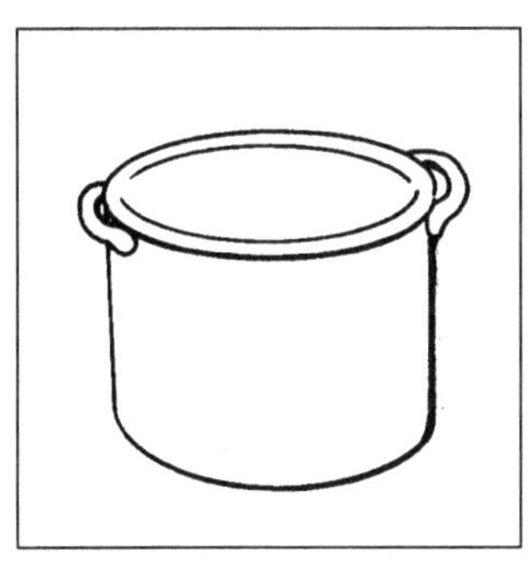

p __ t __ h __ m __

The letters **oa** and **oe** can stand for the long **o** sound.

Circle the picture name.

Write the name.

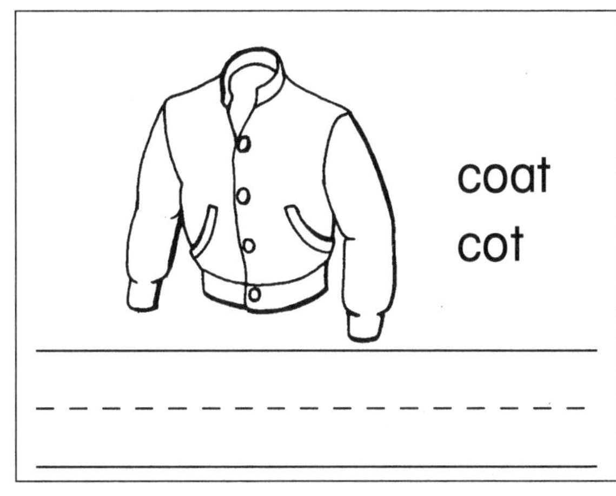

coat
cot

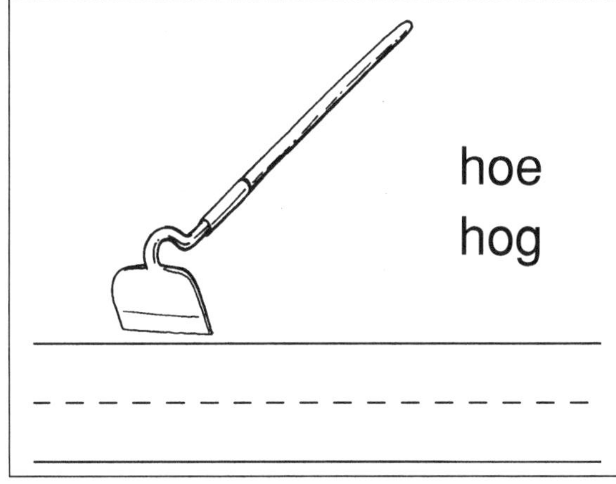

hoe
hog

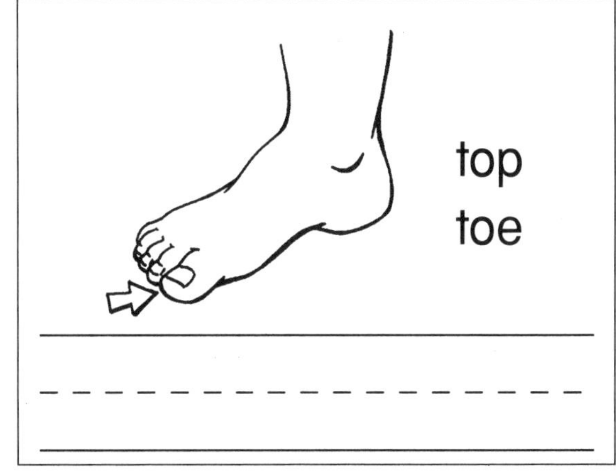

top
toe

Name ____________________ Date ____________________

Circle the words that have the short **i** sound. Put an X on the words that have the long **i** sound.

dime	dice	bib	lid	lips
nine	ice	wig	hill	vine

Draw a picture of a word from the box that has the long **i** sound. Write the name of the picture.

Draw a picture of a word from the box with the short **i** sound. Write the name of the picture.

Name ______________________ Date ____________________

Write the name of the picture with **i_e** if you hear the long **i** sound.

b k

m c

w g

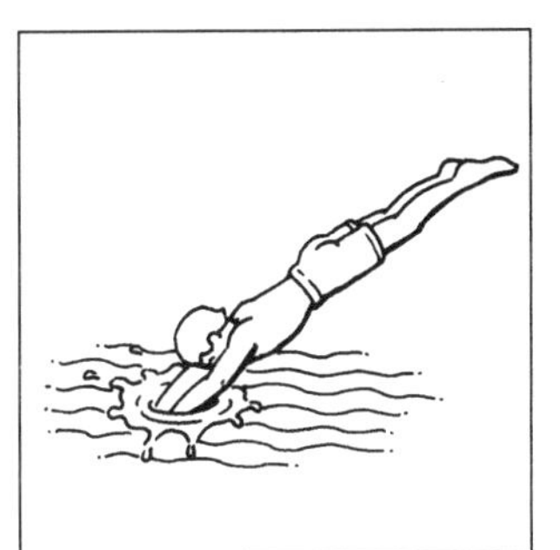

d v

v n

p n

The letters **i_e** and **ie** can stand for the long **i** sound.

Circle the picture name.

Write the name.

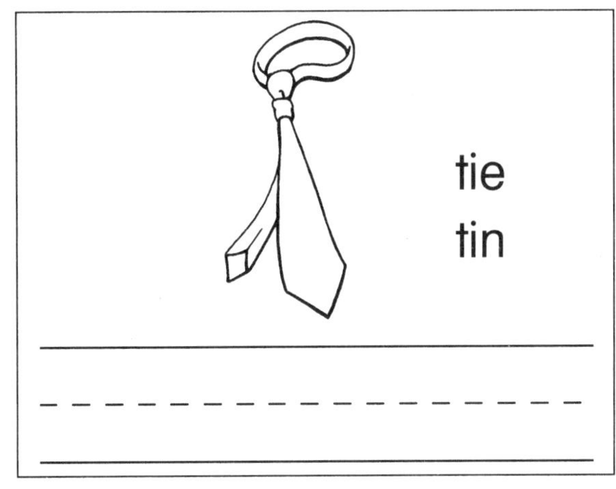

tie
tin

pipe
pig

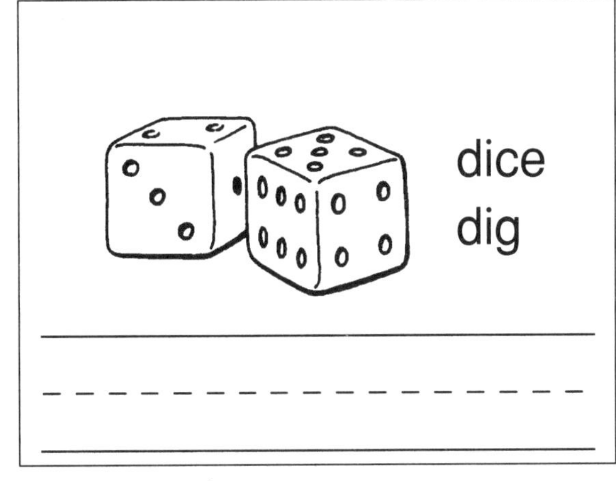

dice
dig

Name ______________________ Date ______________________

Circle the words that have the short **u** sound. Put an X on the words that have the long **u** sound.

tune	gum	rug	cute	mule
cup	sun	fuse	bug	flute

Draw a picture of a word from the box that has the long **u** sound. Write the name of the picture.

Draw a picture of a word from the box with the short **u** sound. Write the name of the picture.

Name ______________________ Date ________________

✏ Write the name of the picture with **u_e** if you hear the long **u** sound.

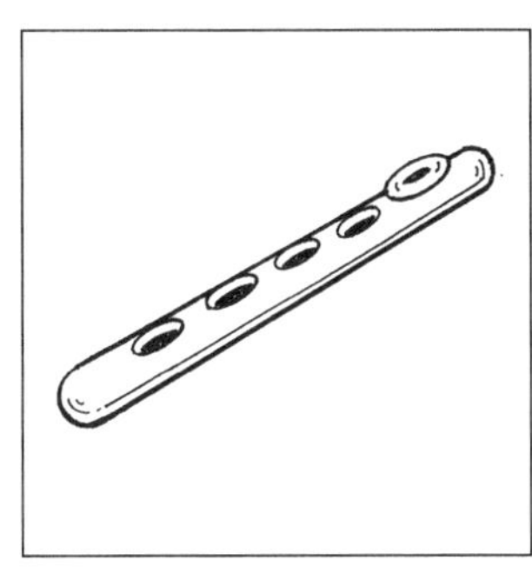

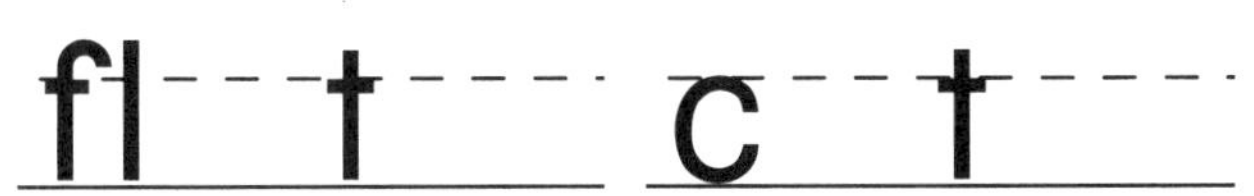

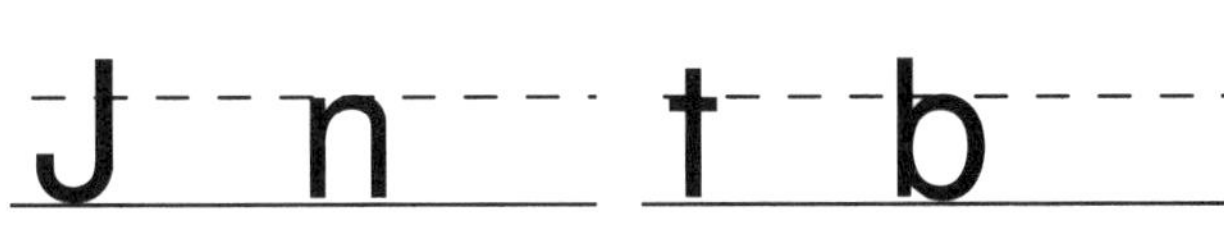

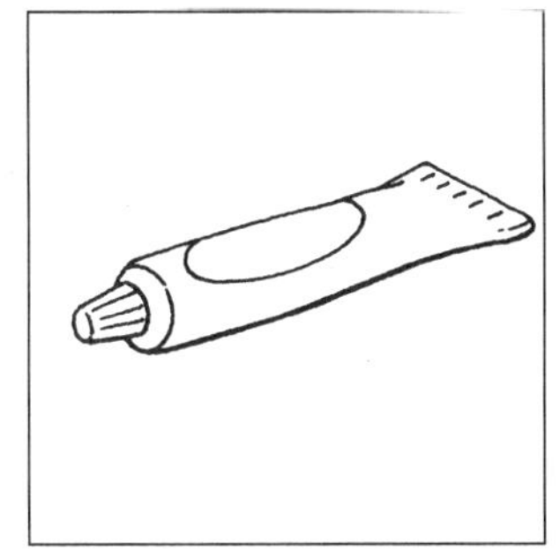

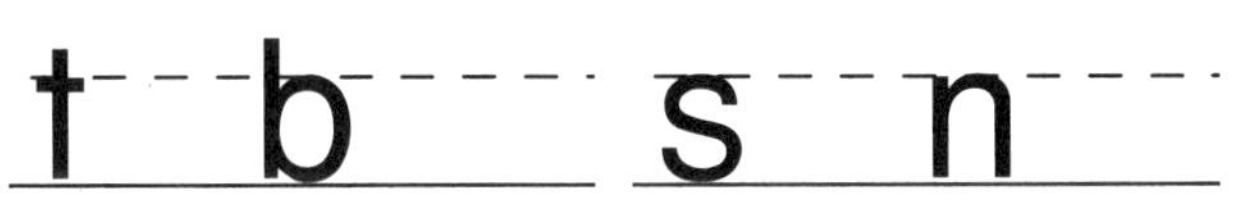

The letters **u_e** can stand for the long **u** sound.

✏ Circle the picture name.

✏ Write the name.

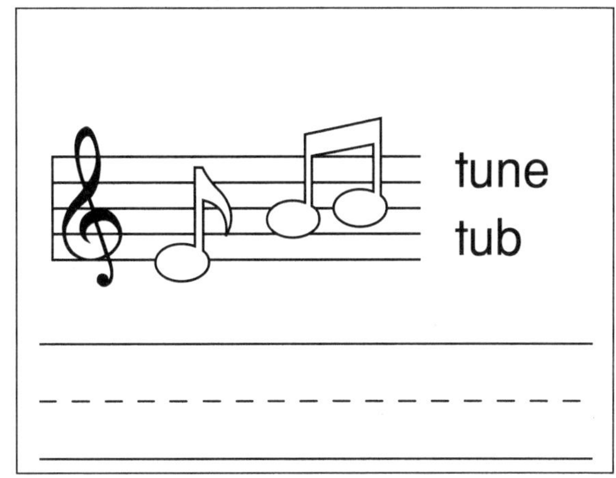

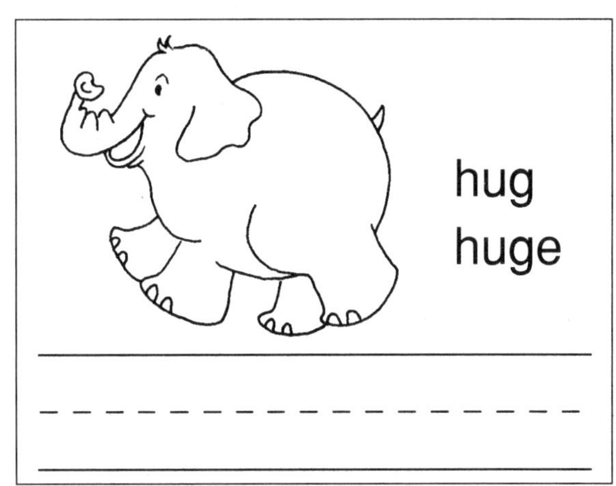

Name ________________________ Date ____________________

Circle the words that have the short **e** sound.
Put an X on the words that have the long **e** sound.

web	egg	see	seal	queen
well	meat	tree	elf	bed

Draw a picture of a word from the box that has the long **e** sound. Write the name of the picture.

____

Draw a picture of a word from the box with the short **e** sound. Write the name of the picture.

____

Name ______________________ Date ____________________

Write the name of the picture with **ea** if you hear the long **e** sound.

b ___ k

s ___ l

t ___ m

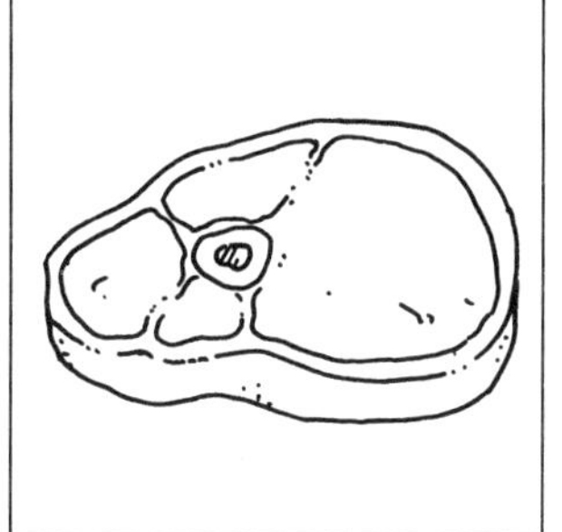

m ___ t

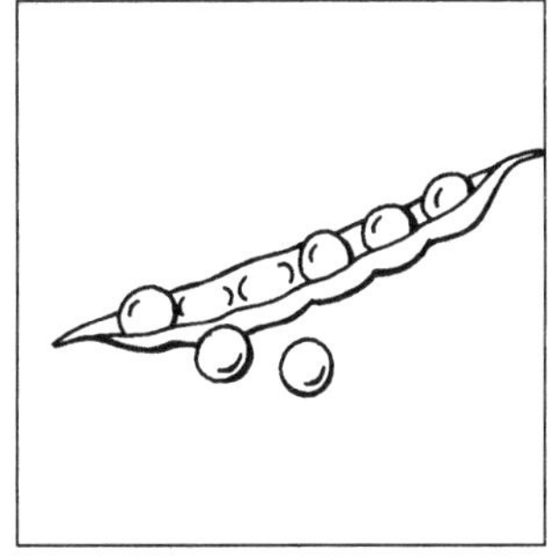

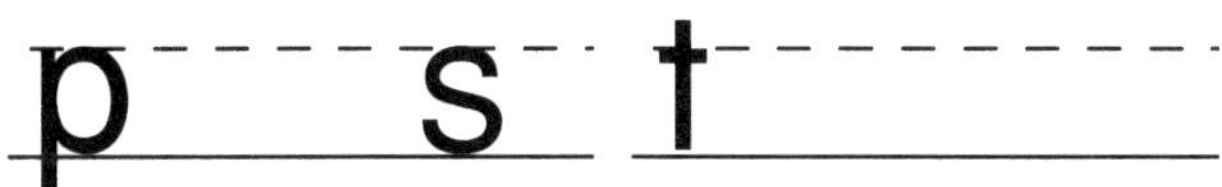

p ___ s

t ___

The letters **ee** can stand for the long **e** sound.

Circle the picture name.

Write the name.

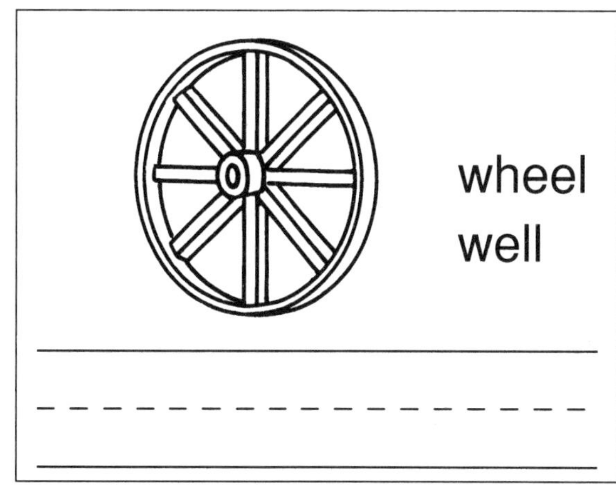

wheel
well

bee
beg

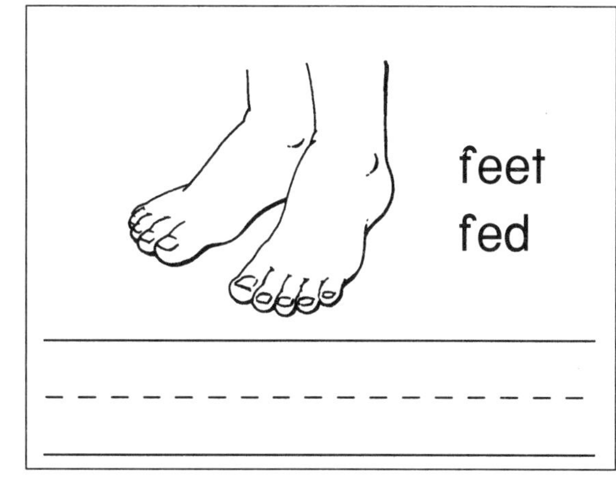

feet
fed

Spelling Words with Long e

Name ______________________ Date ____________________

Read each sentence. Circle the word that completes the sentence. Write the word.

The dog chases his __________.	tail tag
The __________ will eat the oats.	mule mug
The hen can lay an __________.	egg leg
The __________ is in the hive.	beg bee
The blue __________ sits in the tree.	jay day
The __________ swims in the pond.	fish fine
The __________ is on the hill.	got goat

Name ______________________ Date ______________________

Read each sentence. Circle the word that completes the sentence. Write the word.

Kate will ______________ a cake.	**bake** **bat**
Mike likes lemon ______________ .	**pin** **pie**
Tim has a ______________ of milk.	**cup** **cube**
Lee eats ______________ and peas.	**meat** **met**
June plays a ______________ on her flute.	**tune** **tub**
Matt has on a ______________ .	**hat** **hoe**
Joe can dig a deep ______________ .	**hole** **hop**

Name ______________________ Date ____________________

Read and follow the directions. Write the words that are in the dark boxes.

Put an X **above** the house. ____________

Put an X **under** the house. ____________

Put an X **on** the house. ____________

Put an X **beside** the house on the **right**. ____________ ____________

Put an X **beside** the house on the **left**. ____________ ____________

Name ______________________ Date ____________________

Read the sentences. Follow the directions.

1. A happy girl has three balloons. Color the balloons **green**. Color the girl **pink**.

2. The wet seal swims in the pool. Color the seal **brown**. Color the pool **blue**.

3. A big lion jumps through the fire. Color the lion **yellow**. Color the fire **orange**.

4. Two funny clowns get out of the small car. Color the clowns **red**. Color the car **purple**.

5. The brave man stands on a fast horse. Color the man's clothes **green**. Color the horse **black**.

Name ____________________ Date ____________________

Maps can help you follow **directions**.They show which way is north, south, east, and west with the letters N, S, E, and W.

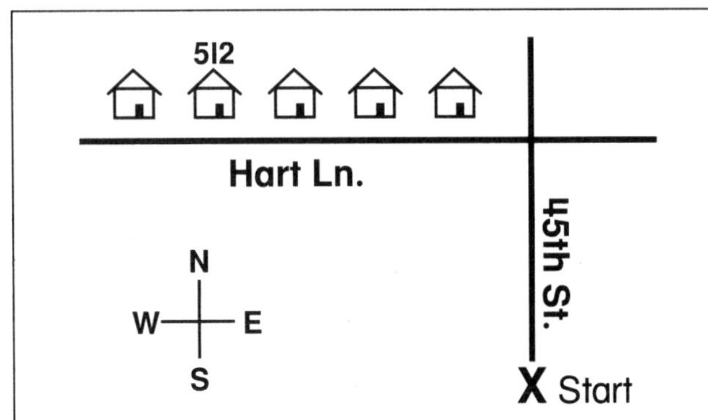

Directions to Ling's house:

1. Go north on 45th Street.
2. Turn west on Hart Lane.
3. Walk west 4 houses to 512 Hart Lane.

Look at the map. Read the directions to Sari's house. Circle Sari's house on the map. Then answer the questions.

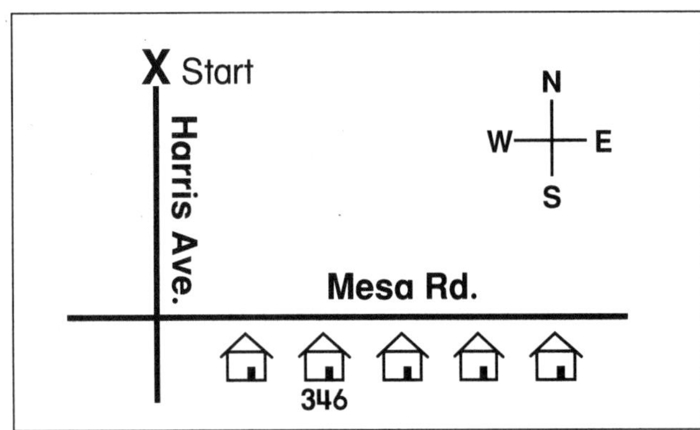

Directions to Sari's house:

1. Go south on Harris Avenue.
2. Turn east on Mesa Road.
3. Walk east 2 houses to 346 Mesa Road.

1. In what direction should you walk first? ____________________
2. On what street should you walk first? ____________________
3. In what direction should you walk next? ____________________
4. On what street should you turn? ____________________
5. When you leave Sari's house, in what direction should you walk to go back to "start"? ____________________

Name ______________________ Date ____________________

Look at each picture. Find the shapes.

Follow the directions to color the pictures.

Color the ▲ yellow.

Color the ■ blue.

Color the ● red.

Color the ▮ and the ▬ green.

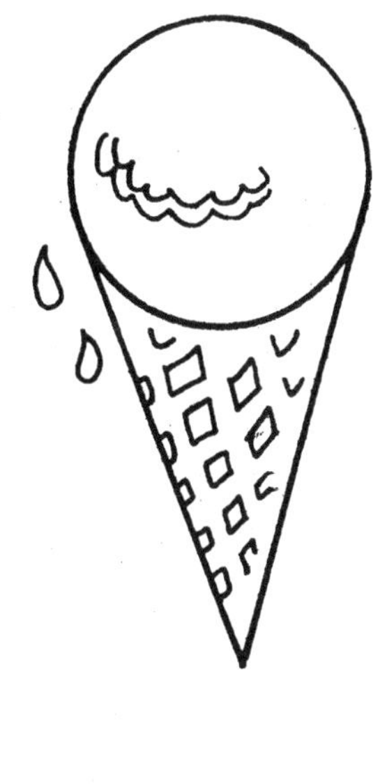

Name ______________________ Date ______________________

Look at the picture of Kim and Todd. Then answer the questions.

1. Who has the larger ball? ____________________
2. Who has the smaller ball? ____________________
3. Whose shirt has longer sleeves? ____________________
4. Whose shirt has shorter sleeves? ____________________
5. Who has longer hair? ____________________
6. Who has shorter hair? ____________________
7. Who is shorter? ____________________
8. Who is taller? ____________________

Name ____________________ Date ____________________

Write the letter of the picture that is different in each row.

   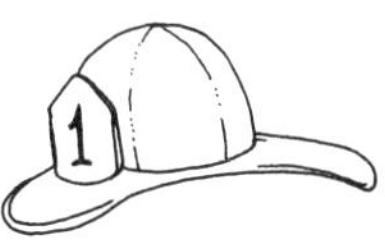

I. a b c d ______

2. a b c d ______

3. a b c d ______

4. a b c d ______

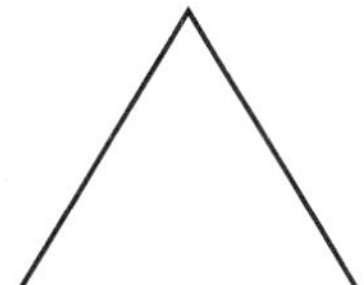 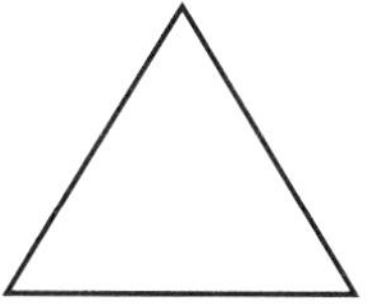 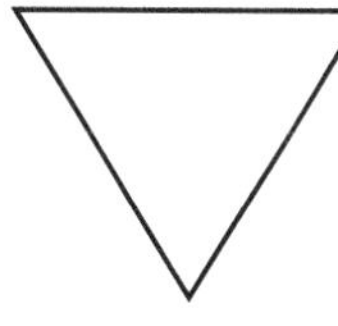 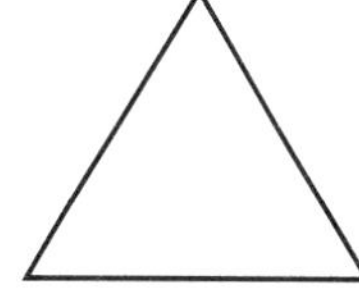

5. a b c d ______

6. a b c d ______

Name ______________________ Date ______________________

✏ Write the word from the box that best fits on each line.

two dogs tail big four long

These animals are ______________. One is small.

The other is ______________. One has short legs.

The other has ______________ legs. Each one has

______________ ears and ______________ feet.

Each has a ______________.

Name ____________________ Date ____________________

Write the number for each picture on a line beside the box where it belongs.

Toy Box

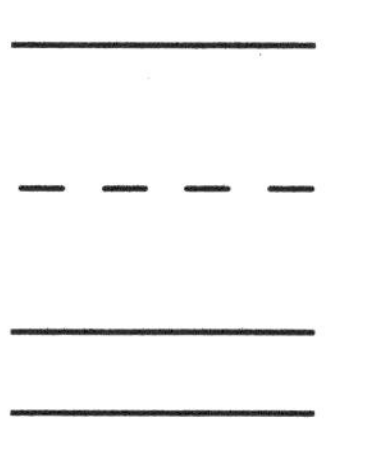

Lunch Box

Tool Box

1. 

2. 

3. 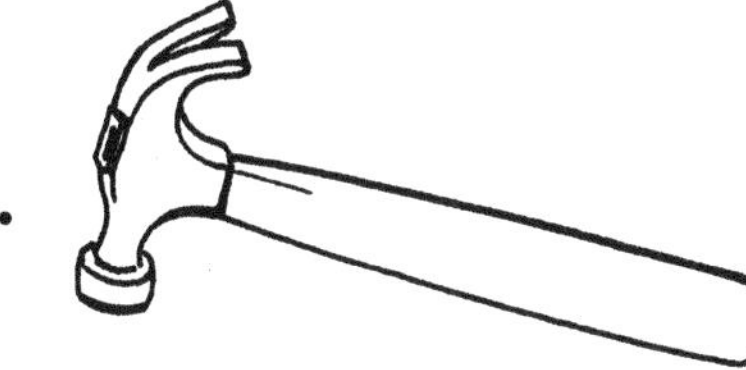

4. 

5.

6. 

Classifying

Name ____________________ Date ____________________

Look at each numbered picture on the left. Find a picture on the right that shows something like it. Write the name of the picture on the line.

1.  ____________________ 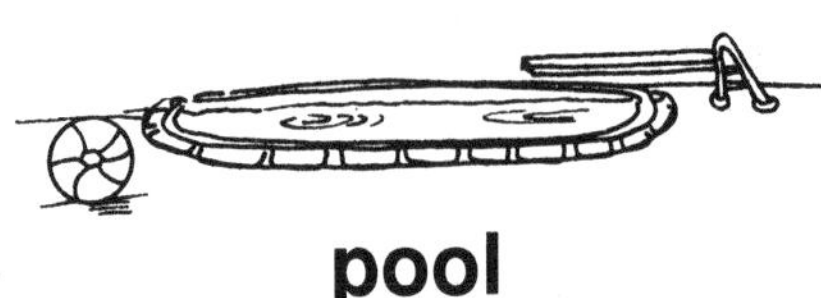 pool

2.  ____________________  car

3.  ____________________  corn

4. 

____________________  parrot

5. 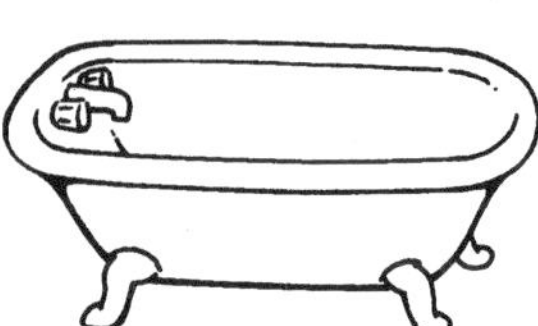 ____________________ hat

Name ____________________ Date ____________________

Read about each picture. Circle the word that names the picture.

1. an animal that hops

rabbit
frog
grasshopper

2. a red fruit

apple
cherry
strawberry

3. a furry animal

dog
kitten
hamster

4. a green plant

tree
bush
grass

5. covers for feet

boots
sandals
sneakers

6. a tool for drawing

pencil
crayon
pen

Name ______________________ Date ____________________

Read the word under each picture. Write the words under the correct meaning.

1. a sea animal

2. a toy to play with

3. something to wear

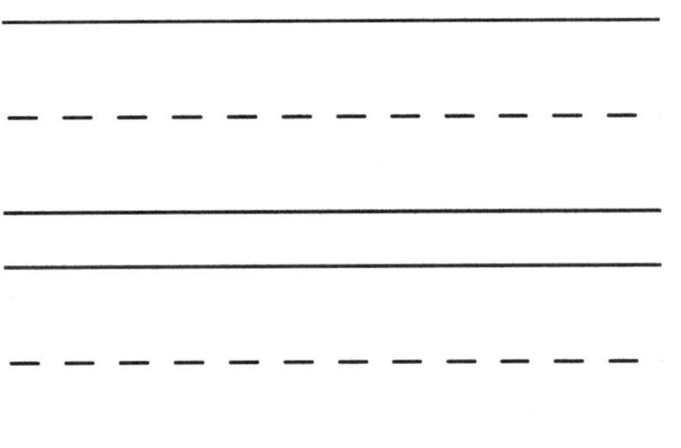

seal

coat

fish

doll

yo-yo

ring

Name ______________________ Date ____________________

Janie and Jenny are twins. ✏ Write the words from the box to tell about each girl.

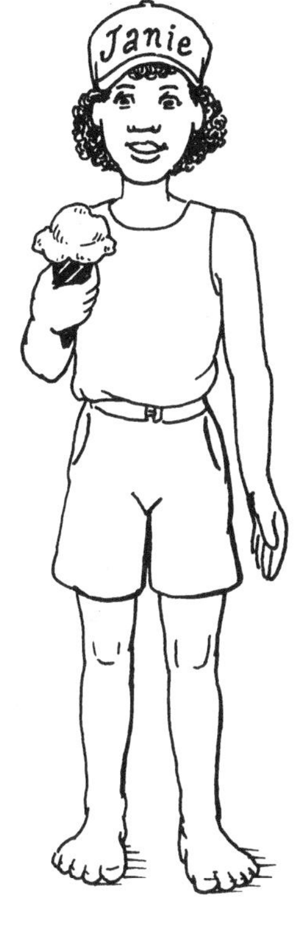

hat
shorts
dress
happy
shoes
no hat
no shoes
sad

Name ______________________ Date ____________________

Read each story. Then write the most important words from the story on the lines. Some are done for you.

1. Sam is a big horse. He lives in a barn. He runs in a field. He eats grass. Sam gives Teri a ride.

is a big horse

____

runs in a field

____

____

2. Shing is a brown puppy. She has a black nose. She lives in the house. She sleeps on a mat. She plays with a ball.

____

has a black nose

____

____

plays with a ball

Outlining and Summarizing/Main Idea

Name ______________________ Date ____________________

Look at the map. Write an answer to each question.

Lee's house

bank

park

pond

store

Jay's house

library

Mia's house

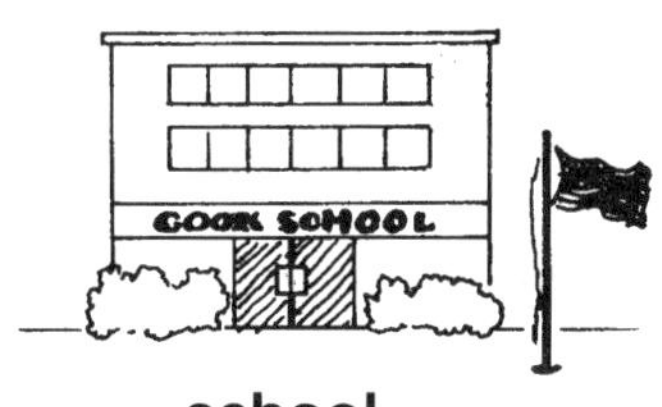

school

1. Whose house is farthest from the school? ______________

2. Whose house is closest to the library? ________________

3. Is the store or the park closer to the pond? __________________

4. Who lives across the street from the park and the school? __________________

Using a Map

Name ____________________ Date ____________________

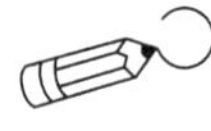 Circle the picture that answers each question.

1. Which hat will fit in the box?

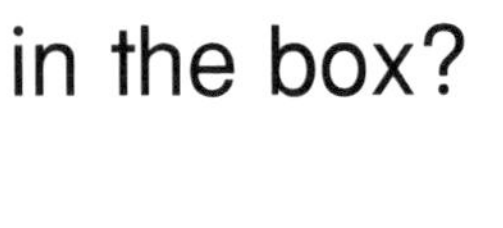

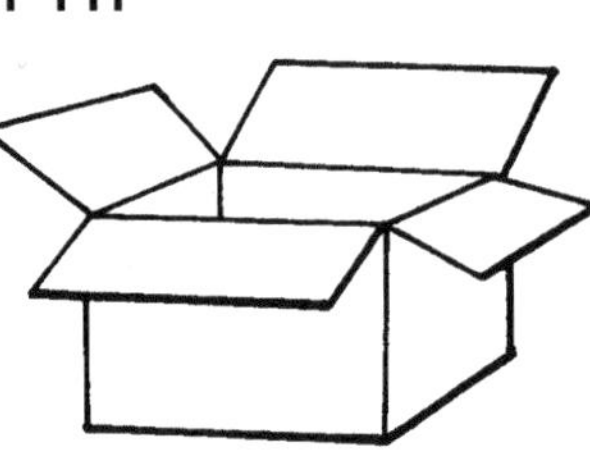

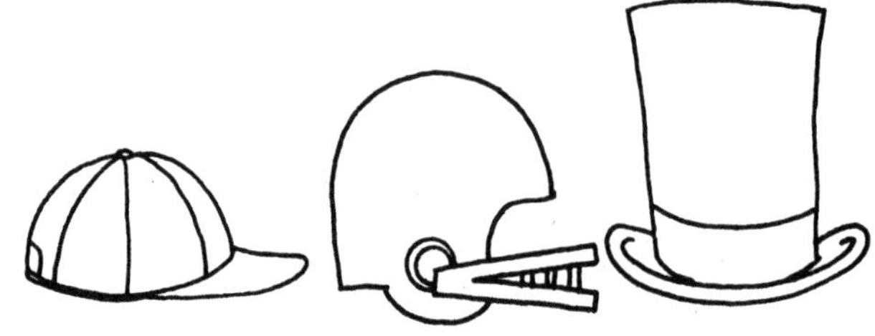

2. Which door is the right size for her?

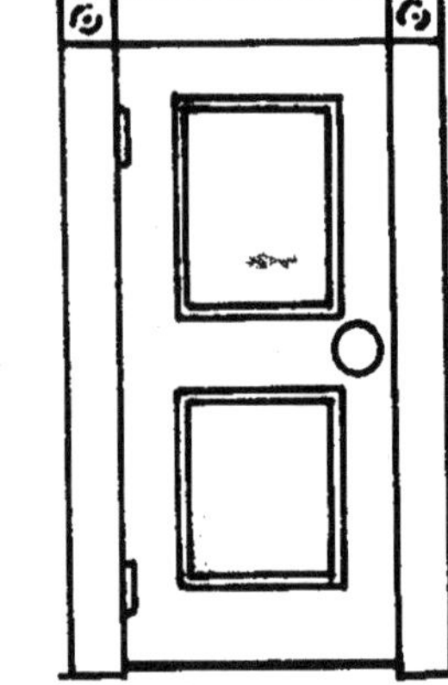

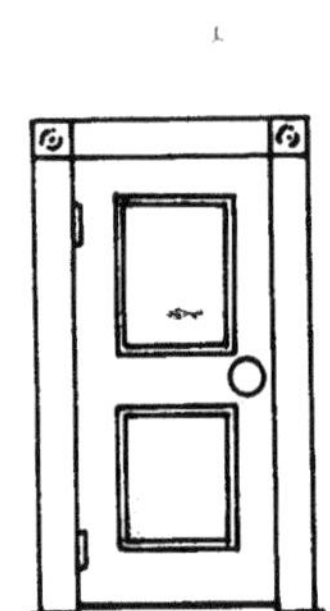

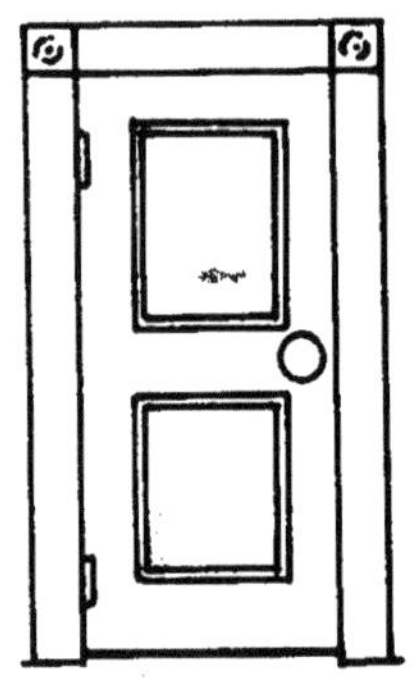

3. Which shoe will fit best?

4. Which doghouse is the right size for the dog?

Name ______________________ Date ____________________

Circle the time that tells how long it probably takes to complete each action.

1. 

5 minutes

9 seconds

2. 

7 hours

10 minutes

3. 

6 days

3 years

4. 

1 hour

3 seconds

Name ______________________ Date ______________________

Read the story. Then number the pictures in order. Use the numbers 1, 2, 3, 4, and 5.

Kristin made a sandwich for lunch. She got two pieces of bread. She put peanut butter on one piece of bread. She put jelly on the other piece of bread. She put the pieces together and cut the sandwich in half. She poured a glass of milk. Kristin sat down to eat her lunch.

Steps in a Process

Name ____________________ Date ____________________

Write 1, 2, and 3 to tell each story in order.

A. ____ Chin and his mother went to the store.

____ They bought a pair of sneakers for Chin.

____ They looked for shoes for Chin.

B. ____ Niki began to play her flute.

____ She got her flute from the case.

____ Niki wanted to play a song.

C. ____ Al made a puppet from the sock.

____ Al found an old sock.

____ He told a story with his puppet.

D. ____ Maria won the game.

____ They played a game of checkers.

____ Maria went to see her friend Tim.

Steps in a Process

Name ______________________ Date ____________________

Say your ABC's. Follow the directions.

✏ Write the letters on the lines.

✏ Write the letter that comes **next**.

R	S	____	B	C	____
J	K	____	O	P	____
D	E	____	H	I	____
L	M	____	U	V	____

✏ Write the letter that comes in the **middle**.

P	____	R	W	____	Y
F	____	H	I	____	K
S	____	U	C	____	E
K	____	M	Q	____	S

✏ Write the letter that comes **before**.

____	B	C	____	G	H
____	X	Y	____	Q	R
____	U	V	____	E	F
____	J	K	____	L	M

Name ________________________ Date ____________________

Put an X on the word that does not belong.

1. green	yellow	purple	run
2. cub	lamb	Sally	puppy
3. ugly	beside	under	between
4. talk	cat	play	swim
5. banana	cherry	grapes	fish

Read the words in the box. Write each word under the name of the group in which it belongs.

angry	**dance**	**sad**	**cake**	**run**	**sandwich**
apple	**cheese**	**give**	**eat**	**happy**	**confused**

6. Feelings	7. Food	8. Actions
____________	____________	____________
____________	____________	____________
____________	____________	____________
____________	____________	____________

Name ____________________ Date ____________________

Names of the days of the week begin with a capital letter.

Example: Tuesday

Write the name of a day to complete each sentence.

1. The first day of the week is ________________.
2. The day that comes before Friday is ________________.
3. The day in the middle of the week is ________________.
4. The day that comes after Monday is ________________.
5. My favorite day is ________________.

The abbreviation of the days of the week begin with a capital letter and end with a period.

Sun.	**Mon.**	**Tues.**	**Wed.**	**Thurs.**	**Fri.**	**Sat.**

Write the correct abbreviation for each day.

1. Sunday ________________
2. Monday ________________
3. Tuesday ________________
4. Wednesday ________________
5. Thursday ________________
6. Friday ________________
7. Saturday ________________

Name ______________________ Date ______________________

Names of the months begin with a capital letter.

Example: March

Abbreviations for months begin with a capital letter and end with a period.

Oct.	July
Sept.	Apr.
Dec.	June
Feb.	Aug.
Mar.	Jan.
Nov.	May

✏ Write the months of the year correctly.

✏ Write the correct abbreviation from the box for each month.

1. january ______________________ __________
2. february ______________________ __________
3. march ______________________ __________
4. april ______________________ __________
5. may ______________________ __________
6. june ______________________ __________
7. july ______________________ __________
8. august ______________________ __________
9. september ______________________ __________
10. october ______________________ __________
11. november ______________________ __________
12. december ______________________ __________

Name ______________________ Date ____________________

Names of the four seasons do not begin with capital letters.
Examples: winter, spring, fall, summer

Write the name of a season to complete each sentence.

1. In _______________, we like to go swimming.
2. In _____________, leaves on the trees turn bright colors.
3. In _______________, we wear coats and hats to keep warm.
4. In ____________, flowers grow and the grass turns green.

What is your favorite season? _______________

Draw a picture that makes you think of that season.

Writing Names of Seasons

Name ____________________ Date ____________________

Words in a sentence must be in an order that makes sense. Write these words in an order that makes sense. Remember to add a period. The first one is done for you.

1. reads Samir books
   Samir reads books.
2. sister My juice drinks
   ____
3. a ball Chang caught
   ____
4. the go to I library
   ____
5. play park at We the
   ____
6. a dog has Ray
   ____
7. paints José picture a
   ____

Name ______________________ Date ____________________

A telling sentence is a group of words that tell something.

Example: Sue fed her puppy.

Circle each group of words that is a telling sentence. Put an X over the words if they are not a sentence.

1. Sue loves her puppy.
2. His name is Shag.
3. Furry dogs.
4. Sue plays with Shag.
5. Chases a ball.

An asking sentence is a group of words that asks a question. You can answer an asking sentence.

Example: How old are you?

Circle the asking sentences. Put an X over the words if they are not a sentence.

6. Do you like dogs?
7. Where is Sue?
8. Why did?
9. Dogs and cats?
10. Can you see Shag?

Name ______________________ Date ____________________

The naming part of a sentence tells who or what the sentence is about.

Example: (Birds) fly in the sky.

Circle the naming part of each sentence.

1. Inez shops for food.
2. Pedro cooks dinner.
3. Manny and Rosa wash dishes.
4. My family and I work together.

The action part of a sentence tells what someone or something does.

Example: Birds (fly) in the sky.

Circle the action part of each sentence.

5. Inez shops for food.
6. Pedro cooks dinner.
7. Manny and Rosa wash dishes.
8. My family and I work together.

Name ____________________ Date ____________________

Write a **T** on the line beside the telling sentences.
Write an **A** on the line beside the asking sentences.

_____ 1. Where is Josh's house?

_____ 2. Josh lives near Katie.

_____ 3. Do you want to play a game?

_____ 4. I like to paint pictures.

_____ 5. Who rides a bike?

 Circle the naming part of each sentence in blue.

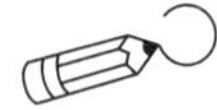 Circle the action part of each sentence in red.

6. My friend goes to the zoo with me.
7. Monkeys climb trees.
8. Tigers roar loudly.
9. Whales swim in the water.
10. The giraffe eats leaves.

Name ______________________ Date ______________________

Words that end with the same sound are rhyming words.

Example: bat-hat rice-mice

Read each word. Find a rhyming word on the ants. Write it on the line.

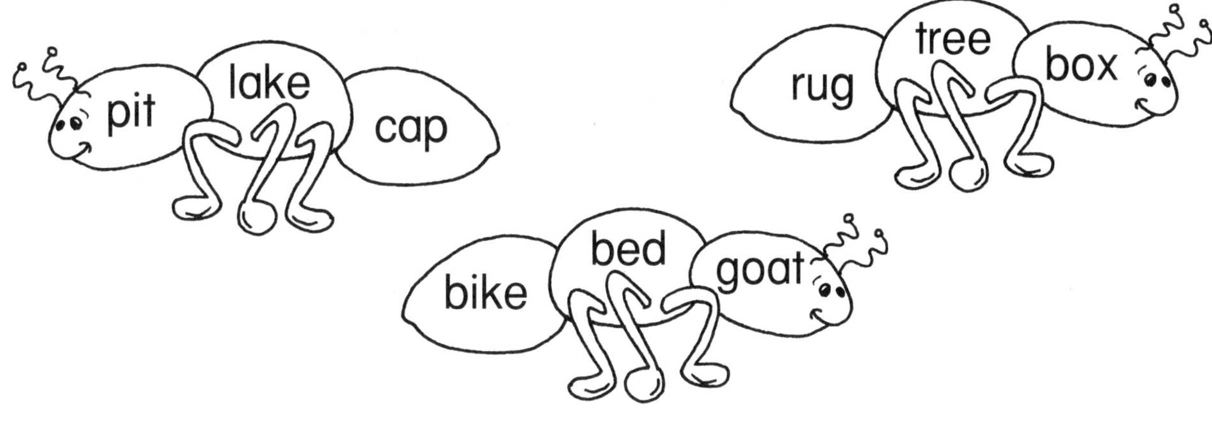

1. bee ______________________
2. kit ______________________
3. boat ______________________
4. bug ______________________
5. map ______________________
6. like ______________________
7. fox ______________________
8. red ______________________
9. rake ______________________

Name ____________________ Date ____________________

Answer each question with a word from the box.

book	crawl	cheese	dirt
break	juice	pour	wear

1. What do babies like to do? ____________

2. What is a good drink? ____________

3. What do you read at the library? ____________

4. What happens if you drop a glass? ____________

5. What is a shirt used for? ____________

6. How do you put milk in a cup? ____________

7. What do you wash from your hands? ____________

Name ____________________ Date ____________________

Read each story. Circle the best title for the story.

1. Raul drives a truck. He goes many places. One day Raul ran over something sharp. He had a flat tire. Raul had to get a new tire.

The Big Truck

Raul Likes His Truck

The Flat Tire

---

2. Twins are brothers or sisters born on the same day. There are different kinds of twins. Chan and Cho are twins. They look alike. Rosa and Rico are twins. They look different.

Chan and Cho

Kinds of Twins

Twins Look Alike

---

3. Tiffany and Steve went ice skating. They had a race across the ice. Tiffany won the race. Steve said, "That was fun! Let's race again."

The Race

Angry Steve

Tiffany and Steve

Name ____________________ Date ____________________

Read each story. Circle the sentence that tells the main idea.

1. We had fun on our shopping trip. I got new shoes. My brother got a new shirt. Then we all went to eat ice cream.

---

2. Mariko brushed her teeth. Then she washed her face and put on her nightgown. Mariko was getting ready for bed.

---

3. When it rains, light shines through the drops. The raindrops split up the colors in light. The colors make a pretty arc in the sky. This is how a rainbow forms.

---

4. Gordon planted a garden. First he planted seeds. He watered the seeds every day. Soon small plants sprouted. Then they grew into flowers.

Name ____________________ Date ____________________

Read each story. ✏ Write the sentence that tells the main idea.

1. Erik is an artist. He can paint beautiful pictures of many things. Erik also makes statues from clay. Many people buy his art. His work is shown in a place called a gallery.

____

2. I read a good story today. It was about two children who found a bank robber hiding in a cave. They told the police about the hideout. The children were heroes.

____

3. When I visit Grandma, she bakes cookies for me. We play fun games. Sometimes she takes me shopping. I like to visit Grandma.

____

Name ______________________ Date ____________________

Read each riddle. Circle the words to answer each question.

1. I live in the water. I can swim fast. I have gills and a tail. Sometimes people try to catch me. What am I?

a duck **a fish** **a turtle**

---

2. It is good to eat. It is cold and sweet. It tastes good when it is hot outside. People like to eat it at a birthday party. What is it?

ice **ice cream** **cake**

---

3. It has a face but cannot see. It has hands but no feet. It tells you something but it has no mouth. What is it?

a clock **a telephone** **a computer**

---

4. Sal and Yong live on Main St. Jerry lives on Market St. Tasha lives on the same street as Jerry. Chad lives next door to Tasha. Chad lives on which street?

Main St. **Market St.** **First St.**

Name ______________________ Date ____________________

Read the story. Circle the words to answer each question.

Reed went to Mandy's house for lunch. They made sandwiches. First they got some bread. Mandy put lettuce and cheese on one slice of bread. Reed put some meat on another slice of bread. Then they put the bread together. While Mandy poured some milk to drink, Reed got out the plates. They were ready to eat.

1. Where did Reed and Mandy make lunch?

Mandy's house **Reed's house** **school**

2. Who poured the milk?

Mandy's mom **Reed** **Mandy**

3. What did Reed and Mandy do first?

poured milk **got bread** **put meat on the bread**

4. What is the best name for the story?

Working Together **Mandy's House** **Reed Can Cook**

Name ______________________ Date ____________________

Read the story. Circle the words to answer each question.

Last week there was a big race at school. The best 5 runners in the class were in the race. They started off in a hurry. Rachel ran fast. Leon ran faster. The other runners were in back of them. Jill tripped and hurt her ankle. Niko stopped to help her. Hector ran closer to Rachel. Then Rachel went faster and passed Leon! She won the race.

1. Which runner tripped?

Niko **Leon** **Jill**

2. Who probably came in second?

Leon **Rachel** **Hector**

3. When was the big race?

at school **last week** **today**

4. What is the best name for the story?

The Big Race **Jill's Ankle** **Niko and Jill**

5. What do you think about what Niko did?

____

____

Name ______________________ Date ____________________

Read the story. Circle the words to answer each question.

It was a hot summer day. People stood on the sidewalk and looked down the street. They could hear music. It got louder and louder. Then a band marched down the street! There were clowns and animals, too. A lady threw candy from a float. Everyone wore red, white, and blue. That night there were fireworks in the sky.

1. What were the people waiting to see?

a parade **a circus** **candy**

2. What was making music?

a marching band **a radio** **clowns**

3. What holiday was it?

New Year's Eve **Fourth of July** **Thanksgiving**

4. What is the best name for the story?

The Big Band **Loud Fireworks** **Fourth of July Celebration**

5. What is your favorite thing to do on the Fourth of July?

____

____

Name ____________________ Date ____________________

Read the story. ✏ Circle the words to answer each question.

It was raining when Maria and Rico woke up on Saturday. They were sad because they could not go outside to play. But it stopped raining after lunch. They put on their raincoats and went outside. Maria splashed her feet in a big puddle. Rico let his toy boat float in a stream of water. "This rainy day is not so bad after all!" said Maria.

1. When did it rain?

Sunday night   **Saturday morning**   **Saturday night**

2. Why were the children sad?

Lunch tasted bad.   **It was Saturday.**   **They had to stay inside.**

3. What is the best name for the story?

The Rainy Day   **The Toy Boat**   **Saturday Morning**

4. Why do you think Maria and Rico like the rain?

____

____

Name ______________________ Date ____________________

Read the story. Circle the letter of the word that best fits in the sentence. Write the word on the line.

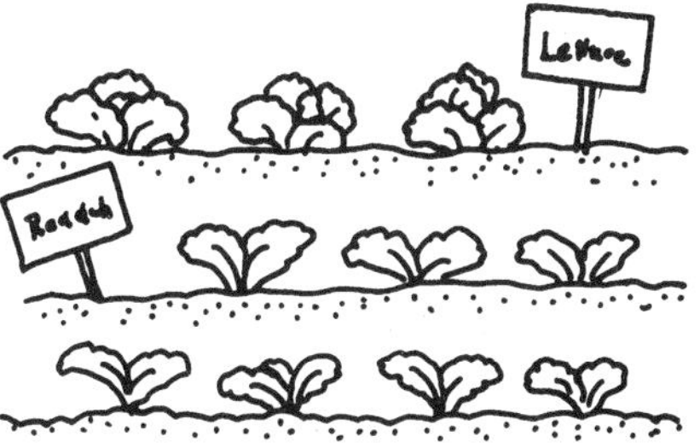

1. **a**. happy	**b**. grow	**c**. rain	**d**. small
2. **a**. food	**b**. water	**c**. friends	**d**. home

Making a garden is easy. You dig holes in the soil for seeds. Then you water them every day. Soon you will see small, green plants. Water makes them ______________________.
1

HINT: When you water plants, does it make them happy? Does the water make the plants grow? Does the water make the plants rain? Does the water make the plants small?

Animals live in different kinds of places. A rabbit lives in a burrow. A bird lives in a nest. A beaver builds a dam. This is where it makes its ______________________.
2

HINT: Why does a beaver build a dam? Does it make its food? Does the beaver make its water? Does the beaver make its friends? Does the beaver make its home?

Name ____________________ Date ____________________

Read the story. Circle the letter of the word that best fits in the sentence. Write the word on the line.

There are many kinds of sports. Playing a sport is a good way to exercise and have fun.

1. **a**. team	**b**. family	**c**. sport	**d**. game
2. **a**. wins	**b**. eats	**c**. plays	**d**. has
3. **a**. soccer balls	**b**. winners	**c**. players	**d**. girls
4. **a**. alone	**b**. well	**c**. sports	**d**. outside

Chin likes to play basketball. He plays with a group called the Panthers. The Panthers are his ____________ (1). They have a lot of fun.

Keisha ____________ (2) soccer. She can hit the ball high in the air. She is on a team called the Stars. Last year they won the most games. They were the ____________ (3).

It is fun to play sports without a team, too. Kelly likes to ski. Brian likes to run. They do not play with a group. They play ____________ (4). They have fun by themselves.

CLOZE: Practice

Name ____________________ Date ____________________

Read the story. Circle the letter of the word that best fits in the sentence. Write the word on the line.

1. **a**. bed	**b**. window	**c**. clock	**d**. floor
2. **a**. wind	**b**. water	**c**. heat	**d**. shade
3. **a**. Art	**b**. Paint	**c**. Noise	**d**. Friends

Stephanie woke up. She did not know what time it was. She looked at the ____________ (1). It was time to get ready for school.

There are many ways to stay cool in the summertime. One thing you can do is to go swimming. You can also sit in the shade with a cold drink. Some people stay indoors to get away from the ____________ (2).

There are many ways to draw a picture. You can use paints or markers. Some people use pencils. You can draw on paper or canvas in many different colors.

____________ (3) is fun to do.

Name ______________________ Date ____________________

Read the story. Circle the letter of the word that best fits in the sentence. Write the word on the line.

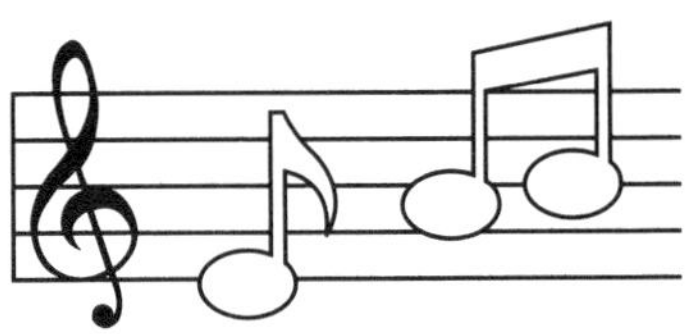

1. **a**. word	**b**. song	**c**. bird	**d**. person
2. **a**. compass	**b**. car	**c**. map	**d**. clock
3. **a**. farm	**b**. jungle	**c**. park	**d**. zoo

There are many different kinds of music. Some music is quiet and slow. Other kinds of music are loud and fast. At a wedding you may hear quiet music. At a party you may hear loud music. Each ___________ (1) sounds different from another.

A ______________ (2) comes in handy. It helps you find out where you are. It tells the names of places and roads. You can use it on trips to keep from getting lost.

A __________ (3) is a fun place to go. There are many different kinds of animals. People come to see interesting creatures from all over the world. Sometimes you can feed the animals.

CLOZE: Practice

Name ______________________ Date ____________________

Read the story. Circle the letter of the word that best fits in the sentence. Write the word on the line.

1. **a**. lighter	**b**. larger	**c**. greener	**d**. younger
2. **a**. friends	**b**. bugs	**c**. horses	**d**. flowers
3. **a**. look	**b**. swim	**c**. sleep	**d**. run

Jason has a stamp collection. He keeps it in a book. He loves to find pretty stamps with interesting pictures. He adds every stamp he finds to his collection.

It is getting ________________ fast.
1

Emil and Kristin like to sit together on the school bus. They help each other with homework. They play games together.

They are ________________.
2

Have you ever gone to the beach? Before you go, you have to get ready. You will need a bathing suit and towels.

You need these so you can ________________ and then dry off afterwards.
3

CLOZE: Pronoun Reference

Name ____________________ Date ____________________

Read the story. Circle the letter of the word that best fits in the sentence. Write the word on the line.

1. **a**. see	**b**. stand	**c**. move	**d**. cry
2. **a**. hungry	**b**. angry	**c**. quiet	**d**. smart
3. **a**. smell	**b**. sound	**c**. taste	**d**. glass

The boy wanted to feed the squirrel. He put some nuts in his hand. He held out his hand. He was very still. He did not

_____________ .
1

Dolphins are friendly animals. Dolphins like people. Dolphins can learn to do tricks. Some dolphins can understand words. They are _____________ .
2

Many people like to drink orange juice. People like to drink orange juice in the morning. People like to drink it with a snack. People drink orange juice all the time. It has a

_____________ people like.
3

CLOZE: Pronoun Reference

Name ______________________ Date ____________________

Read the story. Circle the letter of the word that best fits in the sentence. Write the word on the line.

1. **a**. sad	**b**. happy	**c**. tired	**d**. hungry
2. **a**. homes	**b**. books	**c**. clothes	**d**. food
3. **a**. bikes	**b**. animals	**c**. boats	**d**. homes

Sara was laughing. She smiled at people. She did this because she felt ______________.
1

Reading is exciting. There are many different kinds of______________ . People read to learn about the world.
2
People read to learn about each other. People read for fun. Reading is for everyone.

The wind helps sailboats move in the water. People use paddles to move a canoe in the water. Other ______________
3
have motors to move them in the water. Motors have a lot of power.

Name ______________________ Date ____________________

Read the story. Circle the letter of the word that best fits in the sentence. Write the word on the line.

1. **a**. ears	**b**. feet	**c**. tools	**d**. hats
2. **a**. hungry	**b**. happy	**c**. empty	**d**. ready
3. **a**. call	**b**. leave	**c**. eat	**d**. sleep

Many bats fly at night. They use sounds to find their way. They can hear very well. These bats use their ____________ (1) instead of their eyes.

It is easy to make pancakes. First, mix some milk and eggs. Then add some flour. Stir the batter. Pour some batter onto a hot pan. Then flip the cakes. At last the pancakes are ________________ (2) .

Todd is going camping. He packs some clothes. He puts some food in a sack. He finds the tent. Finally, Todd finds everything. Todd is ready to ______________ (3).

Name ______________________ Date ____________________

Read the story. Circle the letter of the word that best fits in the sentence. Write the word on the line.

1. **a**. rings	**b**. toys	**c**. mittens	**d**. books
2. **a**. friends	**b**. cows	**c**. stars	**d**. clouds
3. **a**. pet	**b**. job	**c**. book	**d**. hat

John is going out to play in the snow. He needs a hat and a coat. He also needs to keep his hands warm. He needs to wear ____1____.

Have you looked at the sky today? What do you see? If it is a clear day, you will see a bright sun and a blue sky. If it is a rainy day, you might see dark ____2____.

Julie is a doctor. She takes care of sick people. She gives people medicine. Julie helps people get well. This is her ____3____.

Name ______________________ Date ____________________

Read the story. Circle the letter of the word that best fits in the sentence. Write the word on the line.

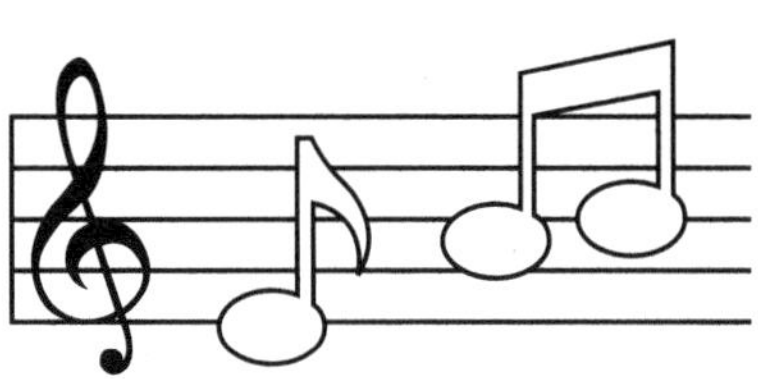

1. **a**. art	**b**. math	**c**. reading	**d**. music
2. **a**. library	**b**. store	**c**. park	**d**. museum
3. **a**. cats	**b**. horses	**c**. birds	**d**. mice

In school we learn about many things. My favorite class is ________________ (1). We sing songs and listen to recordings. We learn to read notes on paper. This is fun. I like to sing the songs I learn for my family.

Rudy had to go to the ________________ (2). He needed some bread and milk. He knew he would find lots of food there. He could buy what he needed and take it home.

What is your favorite kind of animal? Many people like ________________ (3). These animals are furry and playful. They like to sit in your lap and purr. Many people have this animal as a pet.

Name ______________________ Date ____________________

Read the story. Circle the letter of the word that best fits in the blank. Write the word on the line.

1. **a**. water	**b**. sky	**c**. bird	**d**. slow
2. **a**. big	**b**. dry	**c**. near	**d**. fast
3. **a**. small	**b**. wet	**c**. blue	**d**. fish

People go places in many ways. You can ride in planes. These fly very high in the ___________(1). Planes fly far away from the ground. They go very fast. Planes can take you to places that are far away.

You can go places in a car. Cars move on the ground. Cars are better than planes for going places that are not far away. Cars are easy for going places that are __________(2).

Some people go places in a boat. Boats come in many different sizes. Some boats are large and can take many people to places across the ocean. Some boats are not large. They are ____________(3). These boats can take a few people across rivers or lakes. They are not big enough to take many people very far.

CLOZE: Definition Clues

Name ____________________ Date ____________________

Read the story. Circle the letter of the word that best fits in the blank. Write the word on the line.

1. **a**. ready	**b**. light	**c**. pretty	**d**. heavy
2. **a**. water	**b**. herd	**c**. lion	**d**. room
3. **a**. friendly	**b**. mad	**c**. hungry	**d**. cold

Elephants are large animals. They eat a lot of food. They weigh a lot. They are very ________ (1). Even their babies weigh more than a man.

Elephants live together in a group. They stay together all the time. They keep each other safe from their enemies. Elephants do not live alone. An elephant does not leave the ________ (2).

Elephants are nice animals. They greet each other by touching with their trunks. Big elephants help take care of the babies. They are not mean to each other. Elephants are ________ (3).

CLOZE: Applying Skills

Name ____________________ Date ____________________

Read the story. Circle the letter of the word that best fits in the sentence. Write the word on the line.

1. **a**. air	**b**. people	**c**. land	**d**. water
2. **a**. time	**b**. money	**c**. water	**d**. food
3. **a**. animals	**b**. extinct	**c**. small	**d**. people

Whales are the largest animals in the world. They live in the ocean. They do not live on ________(1). They swim deep in the water and come up for air when they need to breathe.

Most whales eat very small animals called plankton. Whales eat them all the time. They have to eat a lot to have enough ________(2).

Some whales are in danger. There are not many left. There are laws that protect these whales. These laws will help keep the whale from becoming ________(3). All of these whales might be gone without the laws.

Name ____________________ Date ____________________

Read the story. Circle the letter of the word that best fits in the sentence. Write the word on the line.

1. **a**. animal	**b**. tools	**c**. person	**d**. book
2. **a**. short	**b**. soft	**c**. fun	**d**. dark
3. **a**. places	**b**. stories	**c**. words	**d**. parts

Computers can be good teachers. You can learn many things with computers. You can solve math problems. You can write stories. Computers are useful ________________ (1).

Some people use computers to play games. You can also make pictures with computers. Computers are not always used for work. Using computers can be ________________ (2).

Many people use computers. People use them at home. People use them at work. People use them at school. There are many ________________ (3) that people use computers.

CLOZE: Applying Skills

Name ____________________ Date ____________________

Read the story. Circle the letter of the word that best fits in the sentence. Write the word on the line.

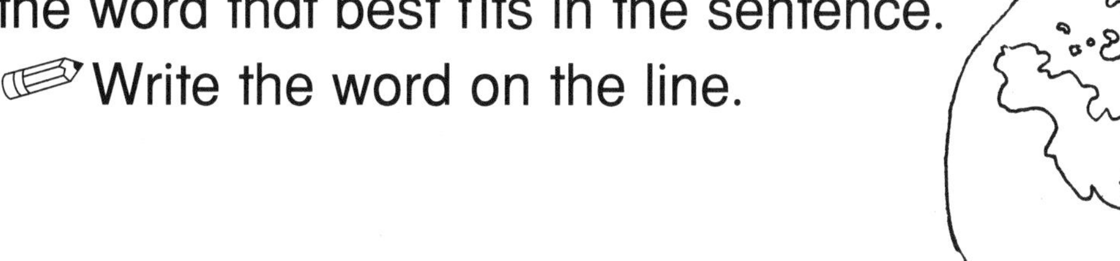

1.	**a**. air	**b**. trash	**c**. person	**d**. time
2.	**a**. sad	**b**. ugly	**c**. hungry	**d**. good
3.	**a**. age	**b**. rule	**c**. school	**d**. book

Waste is everything that we throw away. All of the food, paper, and things that are left over are waste. This is the ______________ (1) that goes to the dump.

Waste is not ______________ (2) for our planet. It can be bad for animals. It can be bad for the air we breathe. Waste makes the world dirty.

If we throw away less, there will be less waste. You can use things again. You can pick up waste from the street. Every person can help. You do not have to be old or young. People of any ______________ (3) can help.

Name ______________________ Date ______________________

Count the tens and ones. Write the number in the box.

There is I ten.
There are 2 ones.

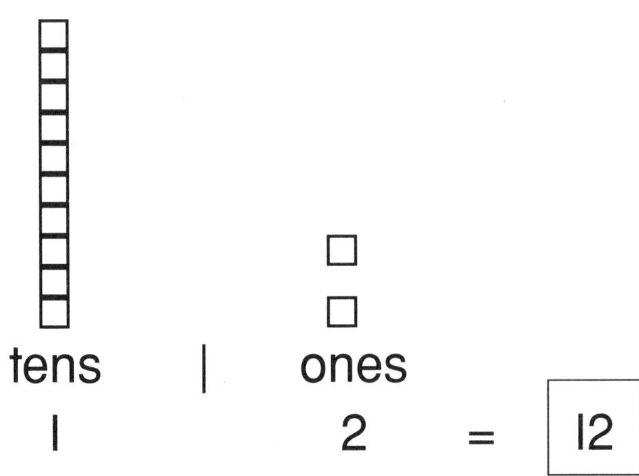

tens	ones		
I	2	=	I2

I.

tens	ones		
___	___	=	☐

2.

tens	ones		
___	___	=	☐

3.

tens	ones		
___	___	=	☐

4.

tens	ones		
___	___	=	☐

5.

tens	ones		
___	___	=	☐

6.

tens	ones		
___	___	=	☐

Name ______________________ Date ______________________

Adding to sums of 11 and 12. How many crayons do you see? Write the number in the box.

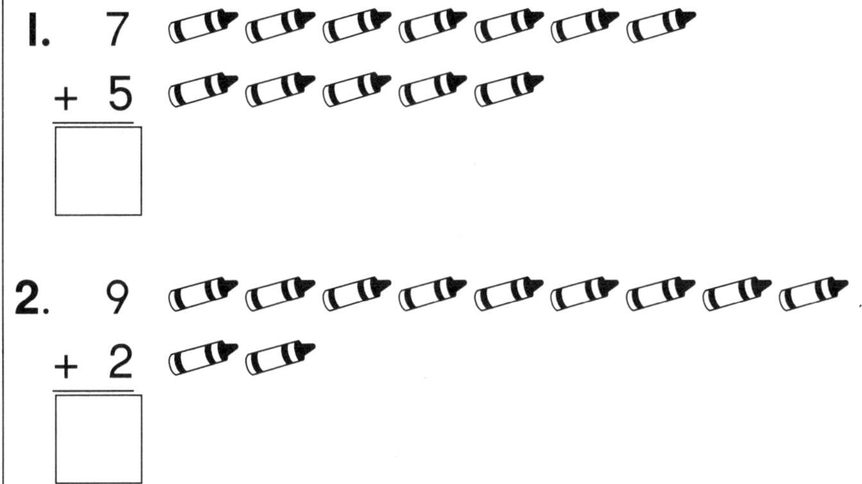

3. 8 + 3 = ☐

4. 2 + 10 = ☐

5. 6 + 6 = ☐

6. 6 + 5 = ☐

7. 9 + 3 = ☐

8. 4 + 8 = ☐

9. 10 + 1 = ☐

10. 7 + 4 = ☐

11. ☐ + 9 = 11

12. 4 + ☐ = 11

13. ☐ + 1 = 12

14. 9 + ☐ = 12

15. Pedro has 9 toy cars. Rita has 3 toy cars. How many toy cars in all? ☐ + ☐ = ☐

Name ____________________ Date ____________________

Adding to sums of 13 and 14. How many [strawberry] do you see? Write the number in the box.

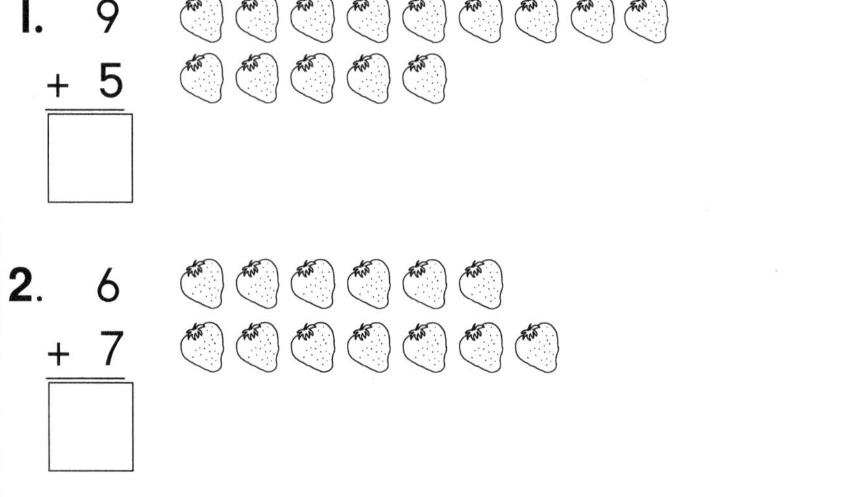

1. 9 + 5 = ☐

2. 6 + 7 = ☐

3. 11 + 3 = ☐

4. 4 + 9 = ☐

5. 3 + 10 = ☐

6. 12 + 2 = ☐

7. 6 + 8 = ☐

8. 4 + 10 = ☐

9. 2 + 11 = ☐

10. 7 + 7 = ☐

11. ☐ + 10 = 14

12. 13 + ☐ = 13

13. ☐ + 9 = 13

14. 1 + ☐ = 14

Name ____________________ Date ____________________

Adding to sums of 15 and 16. How many balloons do you see? Write the number in the box.

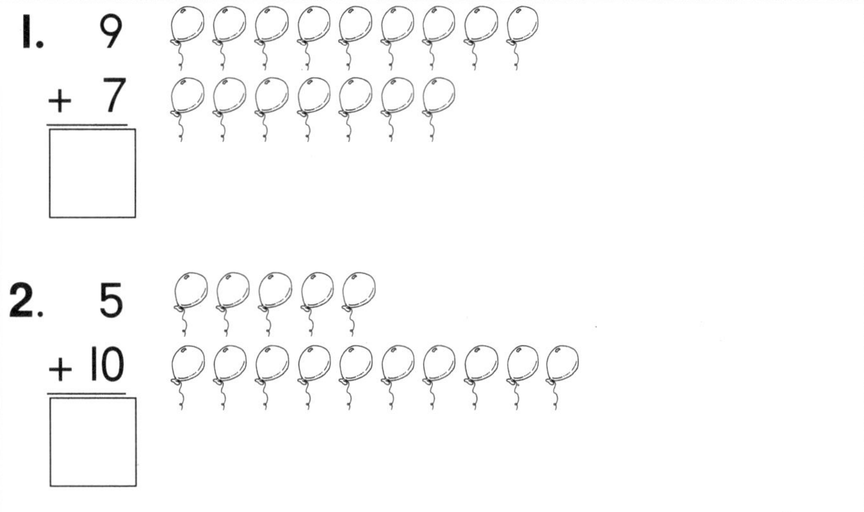

1. 9 + 7 = ☐

2. 5 + 10 = ☐

3. 12 + 3 = ☐

4. 8 + 8 = ☐

5. 6 + 9 = ☐

6. 11 + 4 = ☐

7. 1 + 14 = ☐

8. 0 + 16 = ☐

9. 5 + 11 = ☐

10. 7 + 8 = ☐

11. ☐ + 12 = 15

12. 13 + ☐ = 16

13. ☐ + 5 = 15

14. 14 + ☐ = 16

Nicole has 5 butterflies. If she catches 11 more butterflies, how many will she have in all?

☐ + ☐ = ☐

Name ____________________ Date ____________________

Adding to sums of 17 and 18. How many 🍎 do you see? ✏ Write the number in the box.

1. 12 + 5 = ☐

2. 9 + 9 = ☐

3. 11 + 6 = ☐

4. 8 + 9 = ☐

5. 17 + 1 = ☐

6. 10 + 8 = ☐

7. 2 + 15 = ☐

8. 14 + 3 = ☐

9. 7 + 11 = ☐

10. 6 + 12 = ☐

11. ☐ + 7 = 17

12. 14 + ☐ = 18

13. ☐ + 0 = 18

14. 4 + ☐ = 17

15. Mia has 13 striped beads.
She has 5 yellow beads. How many beads does she have in all?

☐ + ☐ = ☐

Name ____________________ Date ____________________

Adding to sums of 11-19. How many mushrooms do you see? Write the number in the box.

1. 11 + 8 = ☐

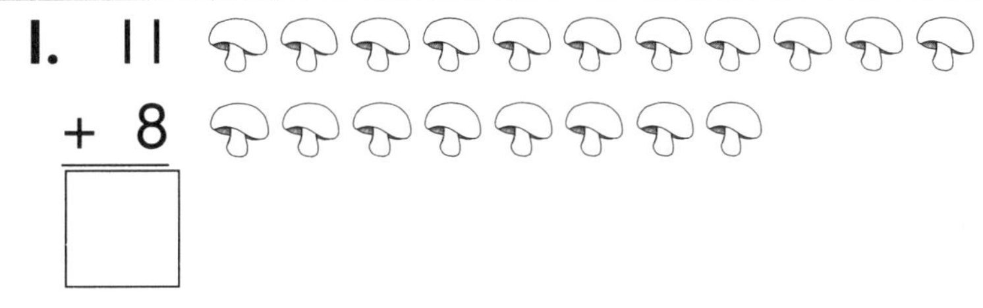

2. 6 + 13 = ☐

3. 17 + 0 = ☐

4. 3 + 15 = ☐

5. 12 + 7 = ☐

6. 10 + 6 = ☐

7. 2 + 9 = ☐

8. 15 + 4 = ☐

9. 3 + 14 = ☐

10. 12 + 6 = ☐

11. ☐ + 5 = 19

12. 6 + ☐ = 11

13. ☐ + 10 = 15

14. 9 + ☐ = 13

15. 3 ants climbed the hill. There were 16 more ants at the top. How many ants are on the hill in all?

☐ + ☐ = ☐

Name ______________________ Date ____________________

Adding. Write the number in the box.

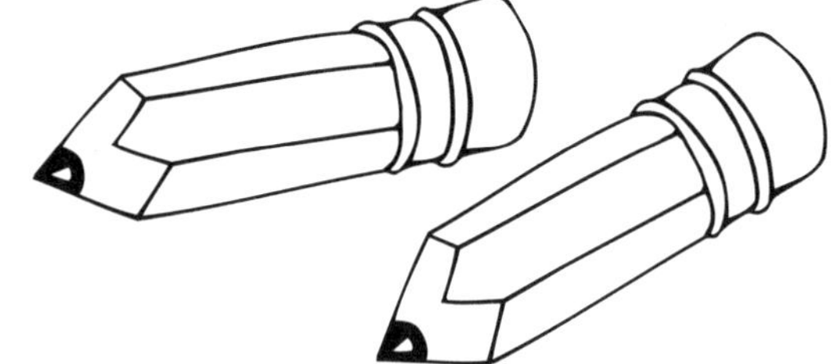

1. 17 + 2 = ☐	2. 4 + 8 = ☐	3. 2 + 6 = ☐	4. 15 + 3 = ☐
5. 9 + 9 = ☐	6. 7 + 6 = ☐	7. 18 + 1 = ☐	8. 10 + 3 = ☐
9. 9 + 5 = ☐	10. 6 + 6 = ☐	11. 7 + 2 = ☐	12. 5 + 14 = ☐
13. 0 + 14 = ☐	14. 3 + 12 = ☐	15. 8 + 10 = ☐	16. 7 + 4 = ☐
17. 4 + 5 = ☐	18. 7 + 8 = ☐	19. 9 + 7 = ☐	20. 14 + 3 = ☐

Name ______________________ Date ______________________

Adding. ✏ Write the number in the box.

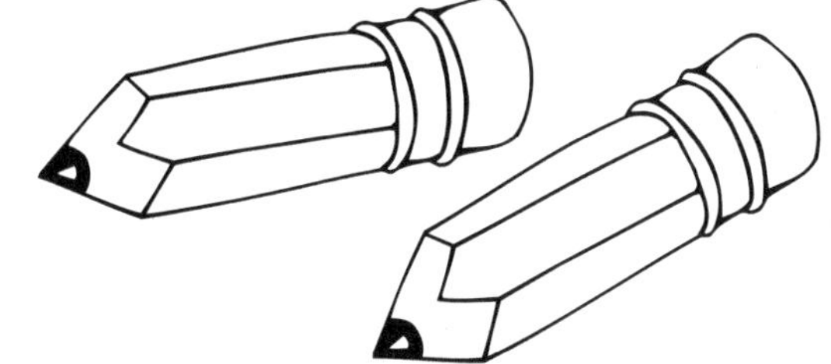

1. 9 + 2 = ☐

2. 14 + 5 = ☐

3. 2 + 16 = ☐

4. 12 + 5 = ☐

---

5. 8 + 9 = ☐

6. 3 + 11 = ☐

7. 8 + 5 = ☐

8. 10 + 3 = ☐

---

9. 4 + 8 = ☐

10. 15 + 3 = ☐

11. 13 + 2 = ☐

12. 8 + 6 = ☐

---

13. 8 + 8 = ☐

14. 8 + 9 = ☐

15. 6 + 13 = ☐

16. 3 + 7 = ☐

---

17. 9 + 7 = ☐

18. 4 + 6 = ☐

19. 19 + 0 = ☐

20. 11 + 2 = ☐

Name ______________________ Date ______________________

Adding. Write the number in the box.

1. 19 + 0 = ☐

2. 15 + 4 = ☐

3. 12 + 6 = ☐

4. 10 + 5 = ☐

5. 3 + 6 = ☐

6. 2 + 8 = ☐

7. 9 + 10 = ☐

8. 7 + 3 = ☐

9. 6 + 8 = ☐

10. 15 + 1 = ☐

11. 13 + 5 = ☐

12. 6 + 2 = ☐

13. 4 + ☐ = 8

14. ☐ + 5 = 13

15. ☐ + 11 = 17

16. 7 + ☐ = 14

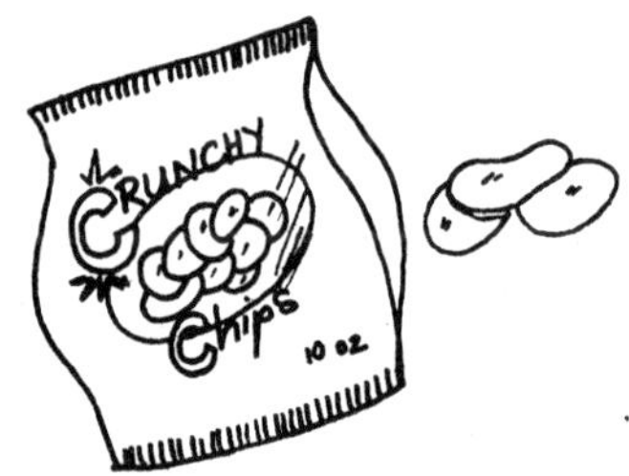

Ed ate 14 chips.
Pat ate 5 chips.
How many chips did the children eat in all? ☐ + ☐ = ☐

Reviewing Addition

Name ____________________ Date ____________________

Subtracting from 10 or less. ✏ Write the number in the box.

1. $10 - 7 = \square$

2. $9 - 3 = \square$

3. $8 - 6 = \square$

4. $10 - 5 = \square$

5. $7 - 5 = \square$

6. $4 - 4 = \square$

7. $10 - 9 = \square$

8. $10 - 2 = \square$

9. $3 - 1 = \square$

10. $9 - 5 = \square$

11. $8 - 7 = \square$

12. $5 - 3 = \square$

13. $\square - 0 = 7$

14. $\square - 3 = 3$

15. $9 - \square = 5$

16. $4 - \square = 2$

Gino had $6. He spent $4 to buy lunch. How much money does Gino have left?

$\square - \square = \square$

Name ____________________ Date ____________________

Subtracting from 11 and 12. How many ⚾ are left? ✏ Write the number in the box.

1. 11 − 6 = ☐

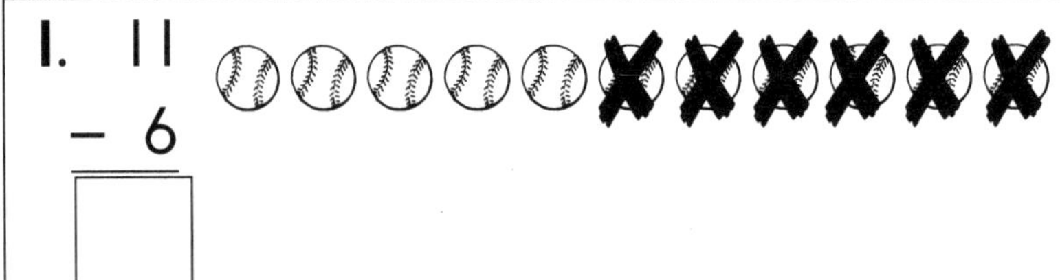

2. 12 − 5 = ☐

3. 11 − 2 = ☐

---

4. 12 − 9 = ☐

5. 11 − 0 = ☐

6. 11 − 8 = ☐

7. 12 − 10 = ☐

---

8. 11 − 4 = ☐

9. 12 − 6 = ☐

10. 12 − 3 = ☐

11. 12 − 7 = ☐

---

12. ☐ − 11 = 1

13. ☐ − 5 = 6

14. 12 − ☐ = 4

15. 12 − ☐ = 8

Name ____________________ Date ____________________

Subtracting from 13 and 14. How many ✏ are left? ✏ Write the number in the box.

1. 13 − 8 = ☐

2. 14 − 7 = ☐

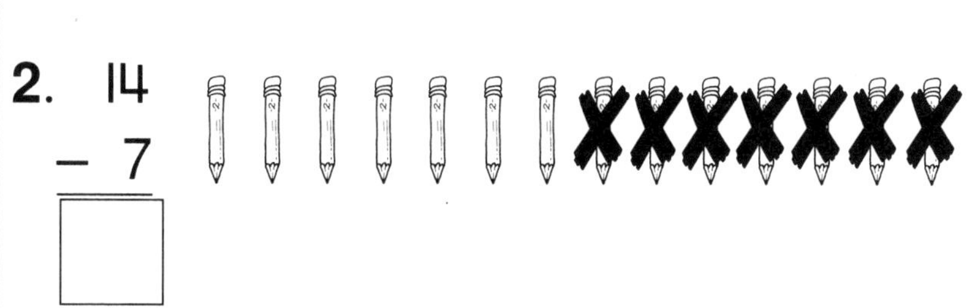

3. 14 − 5 = ☐

4. 13 − 9 = ☐

5. 13 − 11 = ☐

6. 14 − 13 = ☐

7. 14 − 4 = ☐

8. 13 − 6 = ☐

9. 13 − 3 = ☐

10. 14 − 10 = ☐

11. ☐ − 9 = 5

12. ☐ − 2 = 12

13. 13 − ☐ = 11

14. 14 − ☐ = 8

Mia has 13 beads.
She gives away 5 beads.
How many beads does she have left?

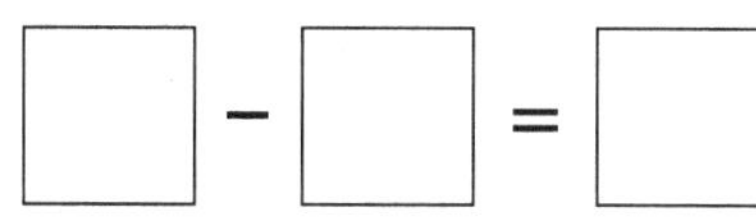

Name ____________________ Date ____________________

Subtracting from 15 and 16. How many bananas are left? Write the number in the box.

1. 16 − 13 = ☐

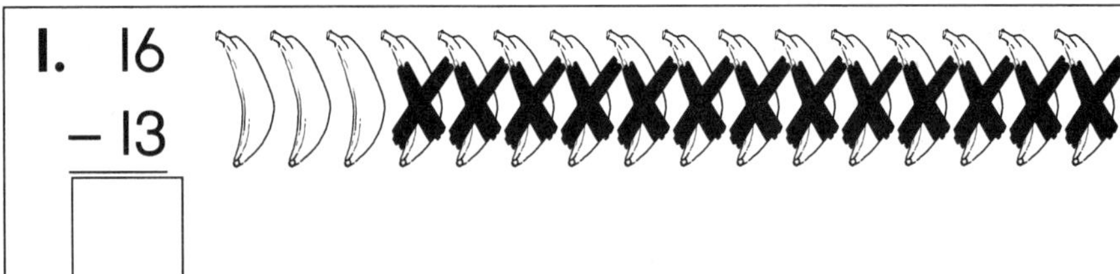

2. 15 − 8 = ☐

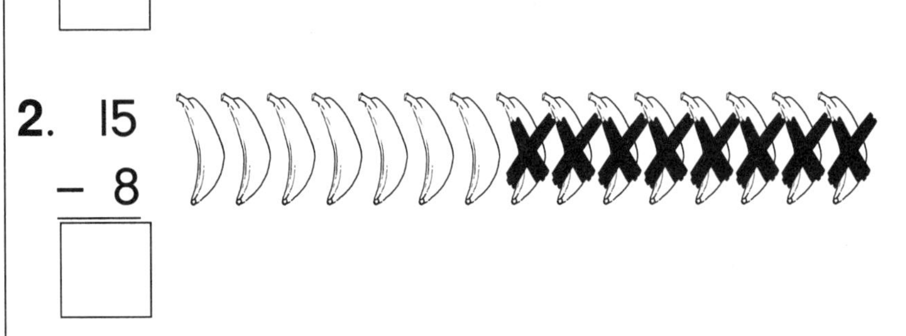

3. 15 − 6 = ☐

4. 16 − 9 = ☐

5. 16 − 15 = ☐

6. 15 − 11 = ☐

7. 16 − 8 = ☐

8. 15 − 4 = ☐

9. 16 − 3 = ☐

10. 15 − 0 = ☐

11. ☐ − 14 = 2

12. ☐ − 2 = 13

13. 15 − ☐ = 8

14. 16 − ☐ = 0

Lee counted 15 stars in the sky. Vic counted 6 stars. How many more stars did Lee count?

☐ − ☐ = ☐

Name ______________________ Date ________________

Subtracting from 17 and 18. How many are left? Write the number in the box.

1. 18
− 15
☐

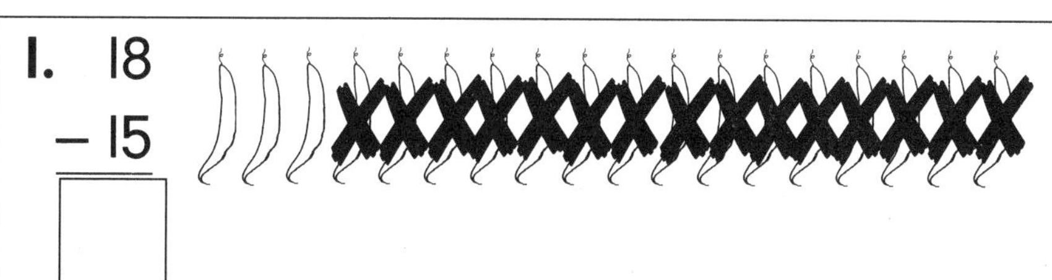

2. 17
− 12
☐

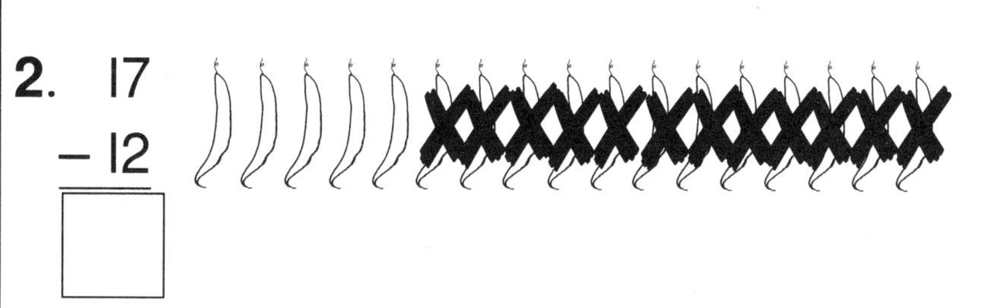

3. 17
− 6
☐

4. 18
− 9
☐

5. 17
− 10
☐

6. 18
− 13
☐

7. 17
− 2
☐

8. 18
− 4
☐

9. 17
− 16
☐

10. 17
− 8
☐

11. ☐
− 7
11

12. ☐
− 5
12

13. 18
− ☐
7

14. 17
− ☐
3

Carrie has 18 party hats. 8 people come to her party. How many extra party hats does she have?

☐ − ☐ = ☐

Name ______________________ Date ______________________

Subtracting from 11-19. How many [paintbrush] are left? [pencil] Write the number in the box.

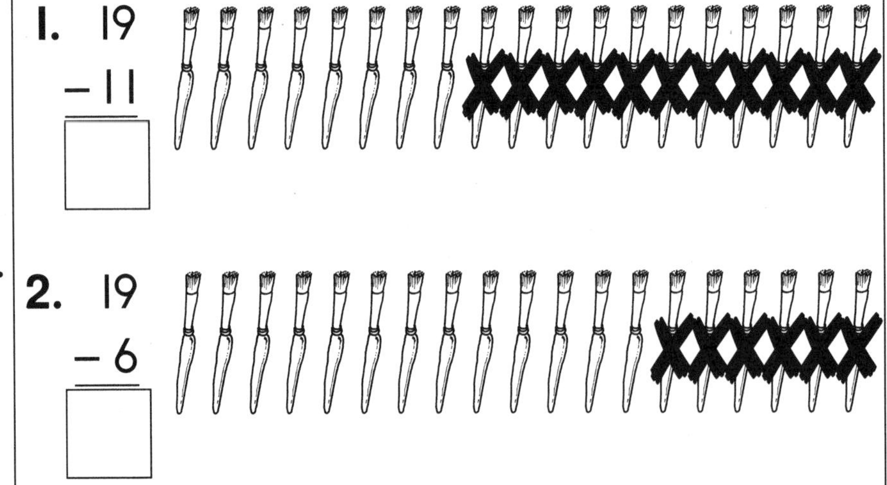

1. 19
− 11
☐

2. 19
− 6
☐

3. 19
− 17
☐

4. 14
− 9
☐

5. 17
− 4
☐

6. 18
− 10
☐

7. 13
− 8
☐

8. 11
− 2
☐

9. 12
− 6
☐

10. 14
− 3
☐

11. ☐
− 18
1

12. ☐
− 14
5

13. 17
− ☐
0

14. 19
− ☐
9

Dr. Garza has 19 lollipops. He gives away 13 lollipops. How many lollipops does he have left?

☐ − ☐ = ☐

Subtracting from 11 – 19

Name ____________________ Date ____________________

Subtracting. ✏ Write the number in the box.

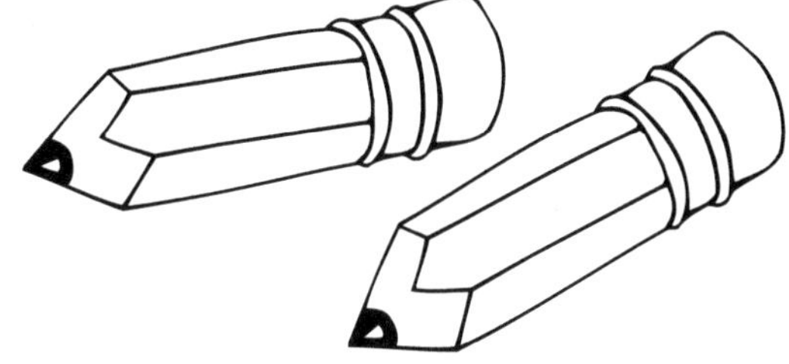

1. 19 − 3 = ☐	**2.** 9 − 2 = ☐	**3.** 10 − 3 = ☐	**4.** 13 − 4 = ☐
5. 13 − 10 = ☐	**6.** 6 − 3 = ☐	**7.** 11 − 5 = ☐	**8.** 12 − 3 = ☐
9. 19 − 16 = ☐	**10.** 8 − 5 = ☐	**11.** 17 − 13 = ☐	**12.** 9 − 3 = ☐
13. 1 − 0 = ☐	**14.** 15 − 13 = ☐	**15.** 5 − 2 = ☐	**16.** 19 − 15 = ☐
17. 16 − 8 = ☐	**18.** 6 − 4 = ☐	**19.** 7 − 2 = ☐	**20.** 19 − 12 = ☐

Name ______________________ Date ______________________

Subtracting.  Write the number in the box.

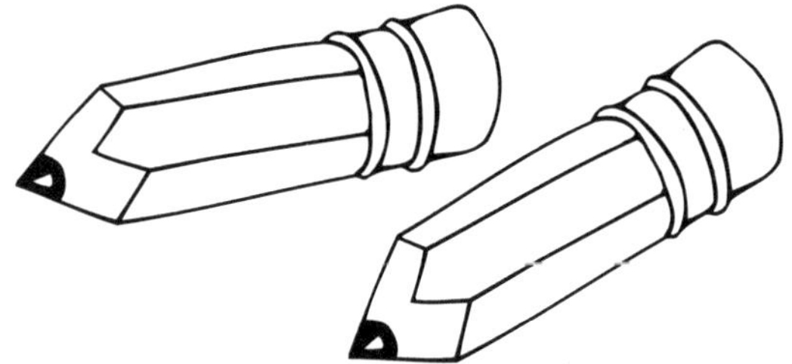

1. 11 − 0 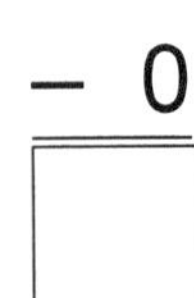	**2.** 4 − 2 ☐	**3.** 17 − 9 ☐	**4.** 14 − 2 ☐
5. 9 − 7 ☐	**6.** 12 − 10 ☐	**7.** 15 − 5 ☐	**8.** 7 − 3 ☐
9. 19 − 5 	**10.** 18 − 17 ☐	**11.** 15 − 8 ☐	**12.** 8 − 2 ☐
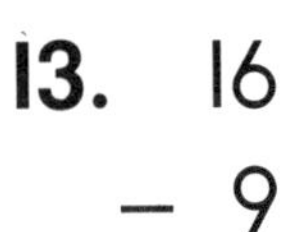 **13.** 16 − 9 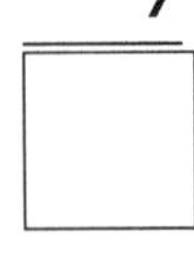	**14.** 19 − 11 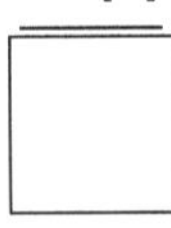	**15.** 4 − 3 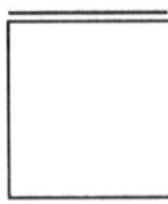	**16.** 10 − 6 
17. 12 − 6 	**18.** 11 − 8 	**19.** 17 − 11 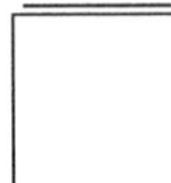	**20.** 19 − 2 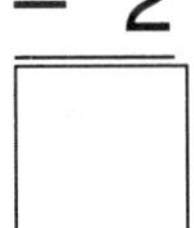

Name ______________________ Date ______________________

Adding and Subtracting. Write the number in the box.

1. 12 + 5 = ☐

2. 14 − 2 = ☐

3. 17 − 3 = ☐

4. 2 + 8 = ☐

5. 19 − 17 = ☐

6. 9 + 6 = ☐

7. 19 − 9 = ☐

8. 12 − 3 = ☐

9. 16 − 12 = ☐

10. 7 − 7 = ☐

11. 12 − 5 = ☐

12. 14 + 2 = ☐

13. 16 + 3 = ☐

14. 8 − 2 = ☐

15. 3 + 13 = ☐

16. 9 + 6 = ☐

Jodi's cat had 5 kittens.
Sari's cat had 6 kittens. How
many kittens do the girls have in all? ☐

They gave away 3 of the kittens.
How many are left? ☐

Name ______________________ Date ____________________

Adding and Subtracting. Write the number in the box.

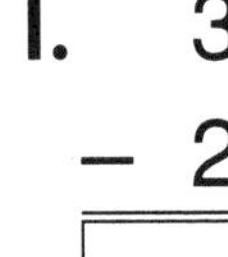
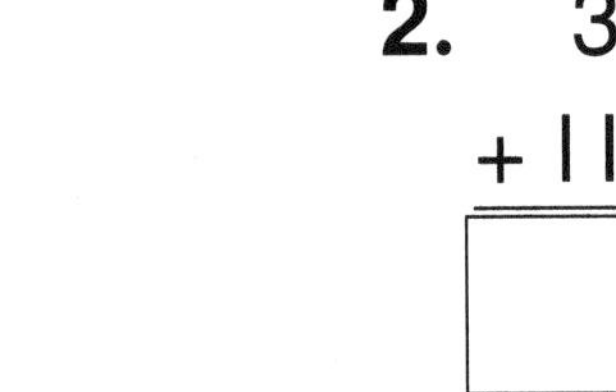

1.	2.	3.	4.
3 − 2 = ☐	3 + 11 = ☐	17 − 11 = ☐	19 − 7 = ☐

5.	6.	7.	8.
9 − 6 = ☐	16 − 9 = ☐	13 + 6 = ☐	11 + 8 = ☐

9.	10.	11.	12.
14 + 3 = ☐	9 − 0 = ☐	12 + 5 = ☐	9 + 9 = ☐

13.	14.	15.	16.
16 + ☐ = 19	☐ − 2 = 15	13 − ☐ = 10	9 + ☐ = 16

NaSha had 12 apples. She gave 2 to Sai and 3 to Dee. How many does she have left?

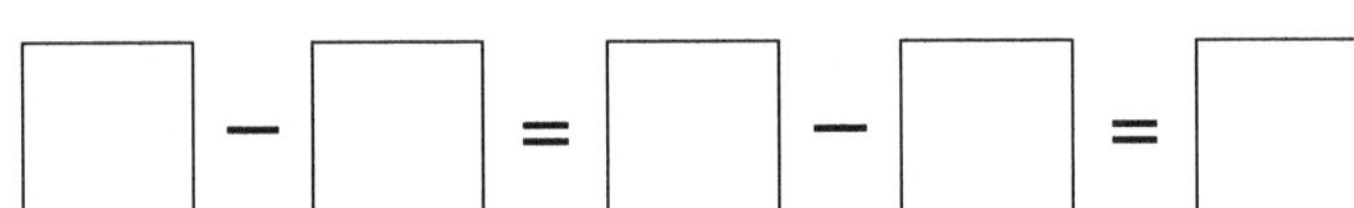

☐ − ☐ = ☐ − ☐ = ☐

Ian had 11 pears. Willie gave him 6 more pears. Ian ate 1 of the pears. How many pears does Ian have left?

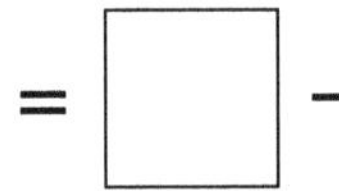
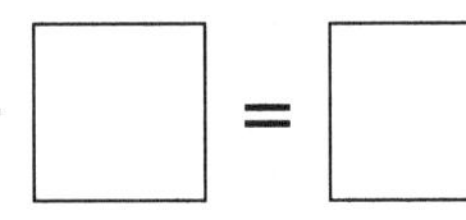

☐ + ☐ = ☐ − ☐ = ☐

Name ______________________ Date ____________________

= 10¢ = 5¢ = 1¢

Count how much money. Write the number in the box.

1. ☐ ¢ 

2. ☐ ¢ 

3. ☐ ¢

4.  ¢  

Add or subtract. Write the number in the box.

5.	6.	7.	8.
4¢	17¢	10¢	14¢
− 3¢	+2¢	− 6¢	+ 3¢
☐ ¢	☐ ¢	☐ ¢	☐ ¢

9. Tori had 18¢. She got a pencil for 9¢ and an eraser for 3¢. How much money does Tori have left?

☐ ¢ − ☐ ¢ = ☐ ¢ − ☐ ¢ = ☐ ¢

10. Tisha had 13¢. She found a nickel.
How much money does Tisha have in all?

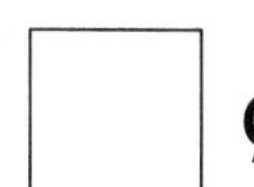 ¢ + 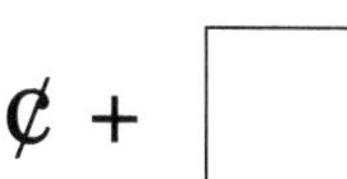 ¢ = 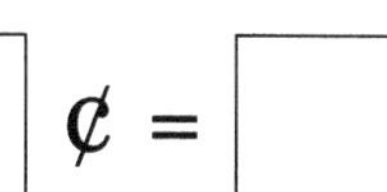 ¢

Circle how much money Tisha has.

Name ____________________ Date ____________________

Read the problem. Write the numbers in the boxes.

1. Marcie is having a birthday party. Her brother made a sign for the party. He used 3 crayons and 4 markers to make the sign. How many colors are in the sign in all?

☐ + ☐ = ☐

---

2. Marcie's mother wants to buy party favors for the party. A whistle is 4¢, a balloon is 2¢, and a horn is 5¢. How much does it cost for these party favors in all?

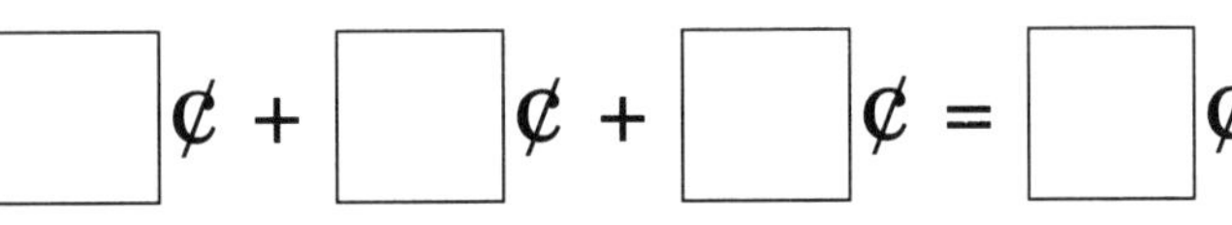

---

3. Marcie has 10 blue cupcakes and 9 pink cupcakes for her party. How many cupcakes does Marcie have in all?

☐ + ☐ = ☐

---

4. There were 12 girls at Marcie's birthday party. There were 7 boys at her party. How many children were at Marcie's party in all?

☐ + ☐ = ☐

---

5. Mick gave Marcie 6 stickers with her present. Niki gave her 4 stickers. Ching gave her 8 stickers. How many stickers did Marcie get in all?

☐ + ☐ = ☐ + ☐ = ☐

---

6. Marcie is 2 years older than her brother. Marcie's brother is 7 years old. How old is Marcie?

☐ + ☐ = ☐

Name ____________________ Date ____________________

Read each problem. Write the numbers in the boxes.

1. 17 children were on the school bus. 9 children got off the bus. How many children are left on the bus?

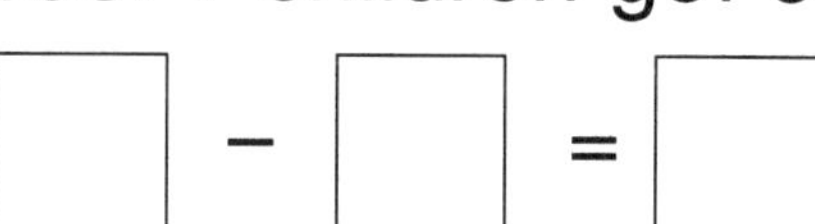

☐ − ☐ = ☐

---

2. 10 children in the class have a cat. 6 children in the class have a dog. How many more children have a cat than a dog?

☐ − ☐ = ☐

---

3. Ellen ate 14 grapes for her snack. Bo ate 12 grapes. How many more grapes did Ellen eat?

☐ − ☐ = ☐

---

4. There are 19 children in the class. 13 children are wearing the school t-shirt. How many children in the class did not wear the school t-shirt?

☐ − ☐ = ☐

---

5. 11 children had apple juice to drink with lunch. 16 children had orange juice to drink. How many more children had orange juice than apple juice?

☐ − ☐ = ☐

---

6. Kim had 15¢. She gave 10¢ to Samir so he could buy a pencil. How much money does Kim have left?

☐ ¢ − ☐ ¢ = ☐ ¢

Name ______________________ Date ____________________

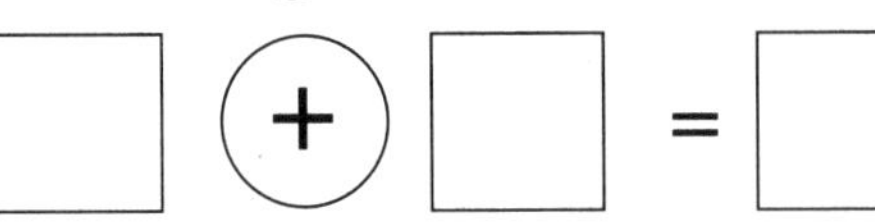

Read the problem. Write + or – in the circle.
Add or subtract. Write the numbers in the boxes.

1. Roy found 4 shells on the beach. Emil gave him 3 more shells. How many shells does Roy have in all?

☐ (+) ☐ = ☐

---

2. 8 girls went swimming at the beach. 12 boys went swimming. How many more boys than girls went swimming?

☐ ◯ ☐ = ☐

---

3. Laura made a sand castle. She put 5 red flags and 4 blue flags on her castle. How many flags did she put on her castle in all?

☐ ◯ ☐ = ☐

---

4. Juan wanted to catch a sand crab. There were 17 crabs on the beach. 14 crabs ran away when they saw Juan. How many sand crabs were left for Juan to catch?

☐ ◯ ☐ = ☐

---

5. Ling got some sand toys for the beach. She got a pail for 19¢ and a shovel for 13¢. How much more was the pail than the shovel?

☐¢ ◯ ☐¢ = ☐¢

---

6. 8 children had red sunglasses. 3 children had pink sunglasses. 5 children had green sunglasses. How many children had sunglasses in all?

☐ ◯ ☐ = ☐ ◯ ☐ = ☐

Name ______________________ Date ____________________

Read the problem. ✏ Write + or – in the circle. Add or subtract. Write the numbers in the boxes.

1. The Garcia family is camping. There are 2 parents and 4 children in their family. How many people are camping in all?

  =

2. José found 6 logs for the fire. Inez found 7 logs. How many logs did they find for the fire in all?

  =

3. Raul toasted 4 marshmallows. Maria toasted 7 marshmallows. How many more marshmallows did Maria toast than Raul?

 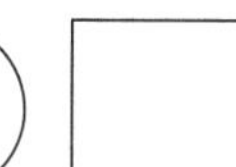 =

4. José went fishing. He got 18 fish. The family ate 14 fish for dinner. How many fish were left?

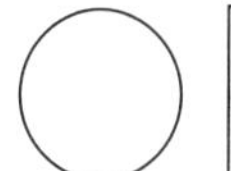 =

5. Maria saw 3 raccoons. Inez saw 5 raccons. Raul saw 7 raccoons. How many racoons did they see in all?

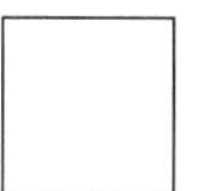  = 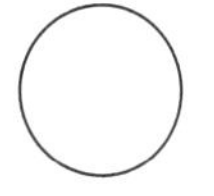 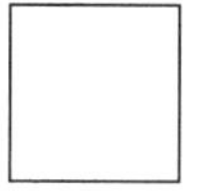 =

6. Inez and Raul went bird watching. They saw 3 robins and 6 blue jays. How many more blue jays did they see than robins?

  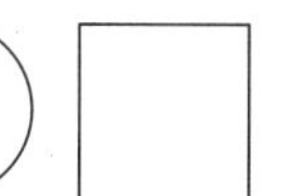 =

Name ______________________ Date ____________________

Add or subtract. Find the pattern.

Write the next problem in each row.

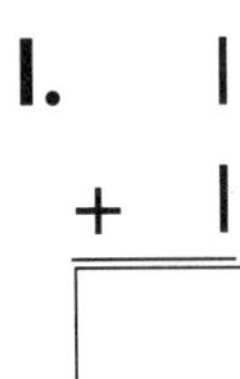

1. 1 + 1 = ☐

2. 2 + 2 = ☐

3. 4 + 4 = ☐

4. 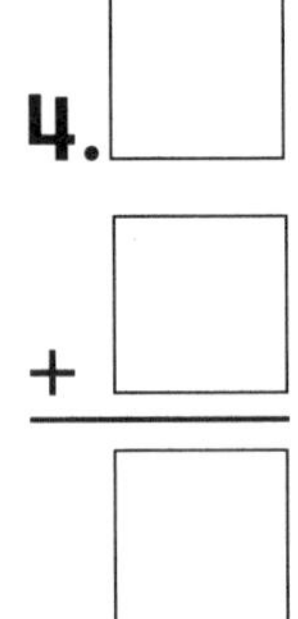

---

5. 4 − 2 = ☐

6. 6 − 3 = ☐

7. 8 − 4 = ☐

8. 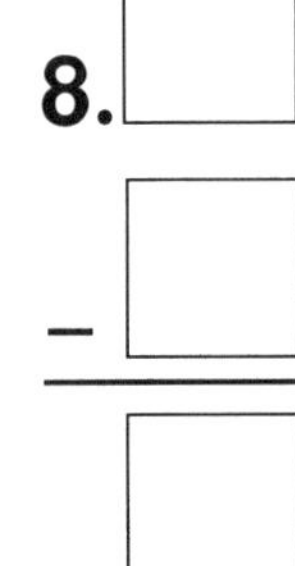

Write the number that is next in the pattern.

Write the pattern.

2 → 4 → 6 → 8

add 2

9. 12 → 9 → 6 → ____

____

10. 3 → 5 → 7 → ____

____

11. 0 → 5 → 10 → ____

____

12. 16 → 12 → 8 → ____

____

Name ______________________ Date ______________________

Add or subtract. Find the pattern.

 Write the next problem in each row.

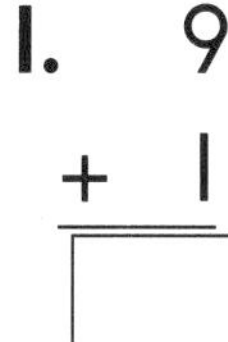

1.	2.	3.	4.
9	8	7	☐
+ 1	+ 2	+ 3	+ ☐
☐	☐	☐	☐

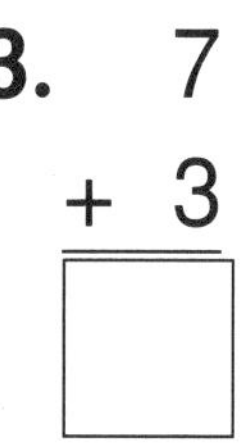

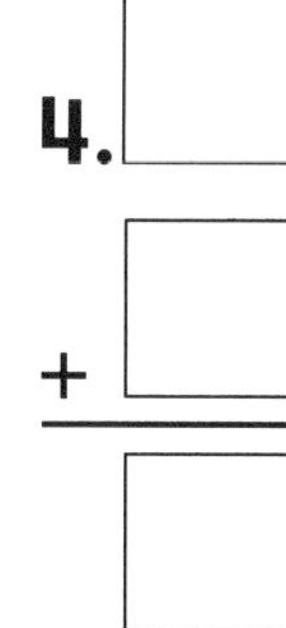

5.	6.	7.	8.
11	9	7	☐
− 2	− 2	− 2	− ☐
☐	☐	☐	☐

Look at each picture. Find the pattern. Circle the shape that is next in the pattern.

9.      

10. 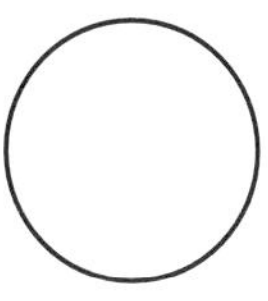 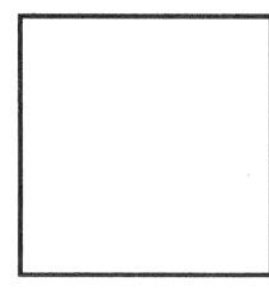 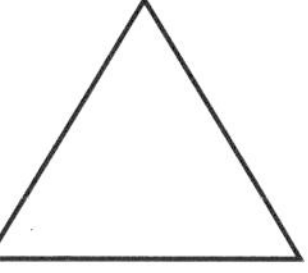 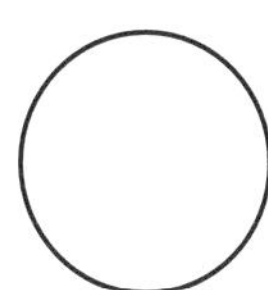 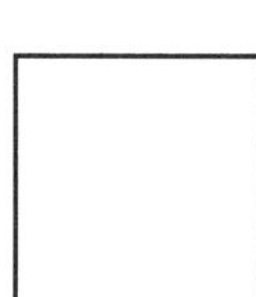 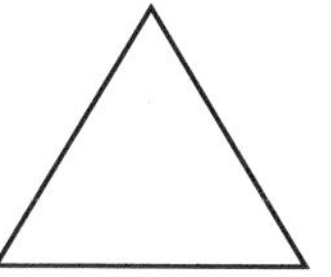

11.   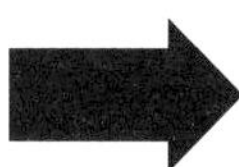   

Name ____________________ Date ____________________

Make a drawing to solve the problem.

1. Heidi planted 15 seeds. 6 did not grow. How many seeds did not grow into flowers?

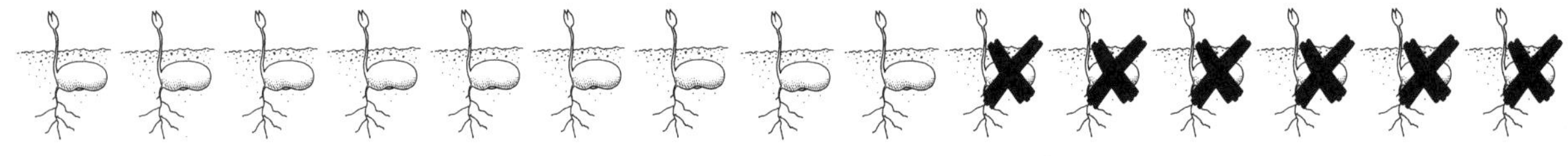

☐ flowers grew.

2. Trina found a bag of marbles. She counted 4 blue marbles, 3 green marbles, and 6 red marbles. How many marbles did she find?

☐ marbles

3. Tony works at a pizza shop. He made 11 pizzas. He sold 8 of the pizzas. How many pizzas were left?

☐ pizzas

4. Manuel collects rocks. He has 14 blue rocks. Leon gave him 4 brown rocks. How many rocks does Manuel have in all?

☐ rocks

Name ______________________ Date ______________________

Make a drawing to solve the problem.

1. There were 13 bees in the tree. 7 bees flew away. How many bees were left?

☐ bees

2. Erica has 3 pairs of socks. She has a red pair, an orange pair, and a green pair. How many socks does she have in all?

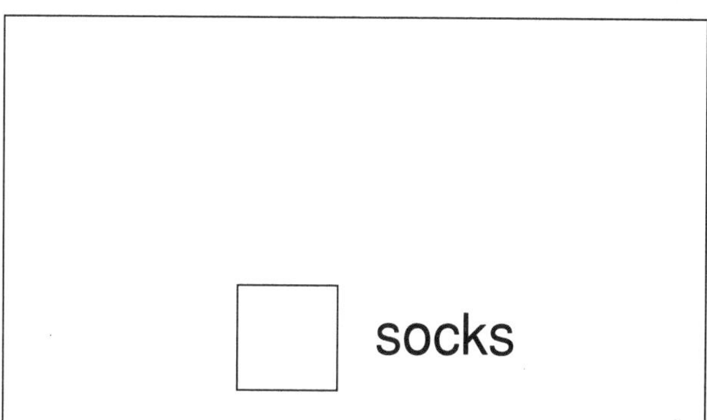

☐ socks

3. Marty and Rudy each have a lemonade stand. Marty sells 6 glasses of lemonade. Rudy sells 10 glasses of lemonade. How many glasses do they sell in all?

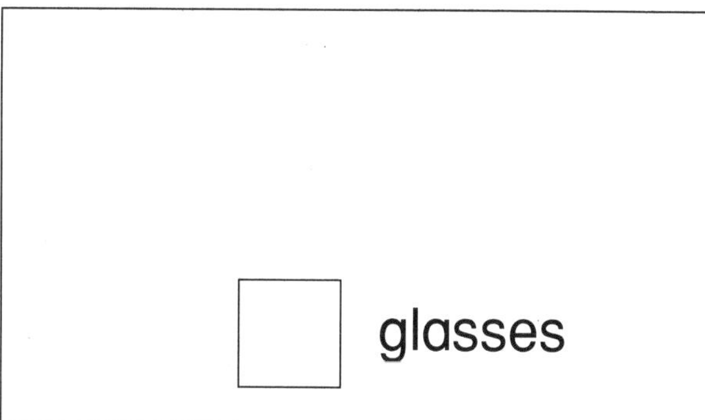

☐ glasses

4. Leroy ate 17 strawberries. Molly ate 12 strawberries. How many more strawberries did Leroy eat than Molly?

☐ strawberries

Name ____________________ Date ____________________

Use the graph to solve each problem. ✏ Write the number in the box.

Mr. Heyworth needed colored paper for his art class. He asked the students to name their favorite color. The graph shows which colors the students liked.

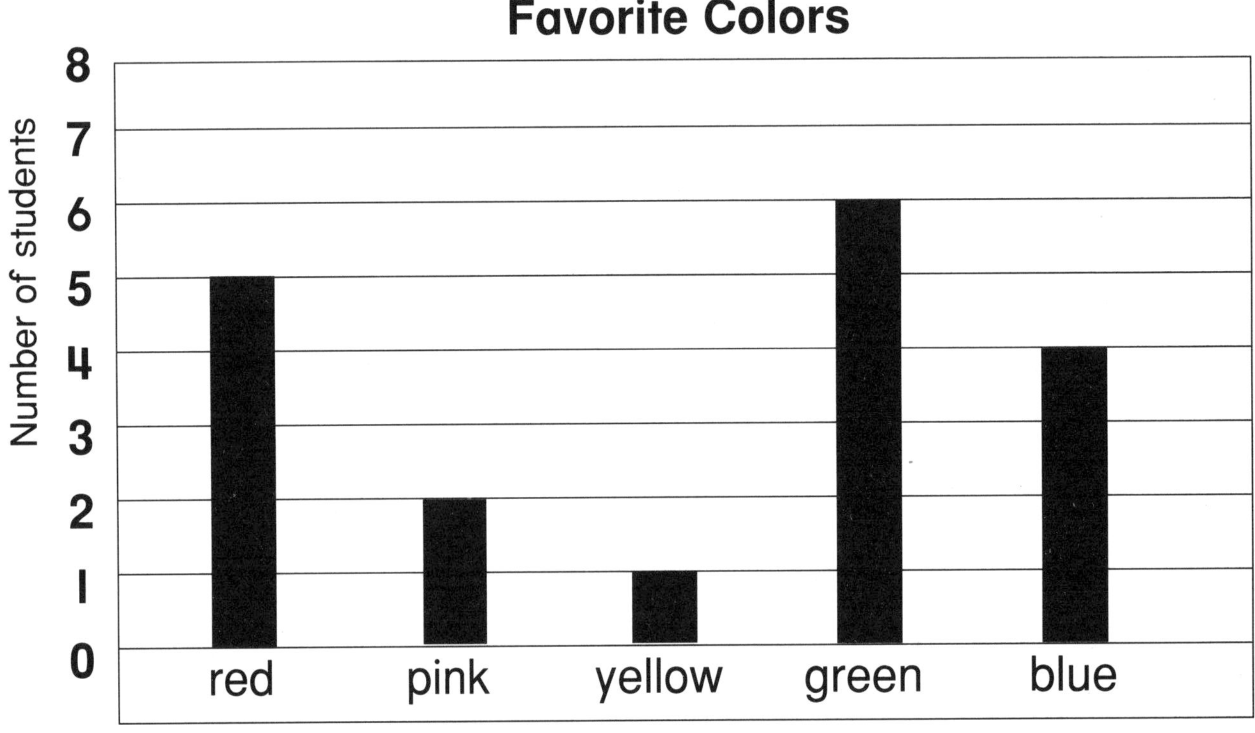

1. How many students chose pink? ☐

2. How many more students chose green than yellow? ☐

3. How many students chose red and blue all together? ☐

4. How many students did not choose green? ☐

5. How many students are in Mr. Heyworth's art class? ☐

Name ______________________ Date ____________________

Use the graph to solve each problem. ✏ Write the number in the box.

Mary has a garden in her yard. She has roses, lilies, daisies, orchids, and tulips. She counted all of her flowers and put the numbers on a picture graph.

Number of Flowers

	1	2	3	4	5	6	7	8	9	10
roses	✿	✿	✿	✿	✿	✿	✿	✿		
lilies	✿	✿	✿							
daisies	✿	✿	✿	✿	✿					
orchids	✿	✿	✿	✿	✿	✿	✿			
tulips	✿	✿	✿	✿	✿	✿	✿	✿	✿	✿

Each ✿ = 1 flower

1. How many daisies does Mary have? ☐

2. How many more roses than orchids does she have? ☐

3. Which flower grows the most in her garden? __________

4. Which flower grows the least? __________

5. How many daisies and orchids does she have in all? ☐

Using Graphs

Name ______________________ Date ____________________

Write a number sentence to solve each problem.

Ricky and Felipe went to Mac's hamburger stand for lunch. Ricky ate 18 french fries with his burger. Felipe ate 12 french fries. How many more fries did Ricky eat than Felipe?

[18] french fries (−) [12] french fries = [6] more fries.

1. Reuben's sandwich shop sold 16 ham sandwiches at lunch. They sold 13 turkey sandwiches. How many more ham sandwiches did they sell?

[ ] ham ( ) [ ] turkey = [ ] more ham

2. Teri ate 4 cookies for dessert. Keith ate 5 cookies. How many cookies did they eat in all?

[ ] ________ ( ) [ ] ________ = [ ] ________

3. The soda shop had 19 cherry sodas. They sold 13 cherry sodas at lunch. How many sodas are left?

[ ] ________ ( ) [ ] ________ = [ ] ________

4. In Ms. Dunn's class, 12 people had a sack lunch. 5 people got a hot lunch in the cafeteria. How many people had lunch in all?

[ ] ________ ( ) [ ] ________ = [ ] ________

Name ______________________ Date ______________________

✏ Write a number sentence to solve each problem.

1. The pet store had 14 birds. They sold 8 birds. How many birds were left?

☐ ________ ◯ ☐ ________ = ☐ ________

---

2. Ronnie has 2 pet rabbits. The mother rabbit had 7 baby bunnies. How many rabbits does he have in all?

☐ ________ ◯ ☐ ________ = ☐ ________

---

3. Jorge has 3 white mice and 6 brown mice. How many mice does he have in all?

☐ ________ ◯ ☐ ________ = ☐ ________

---

4. Gloria's class has an aquarium. There are 13 angel fish and 18 goldfish in the aquarium. How many more goldfish than angel fish are there?

☐ ________ ◯ ☐ ________ = ☐ ________

Name ____________________ Date ____________________

= 10¢ 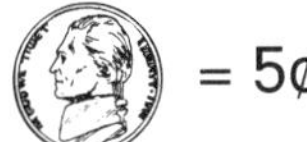 = 5¢  = 1¢

The school store sells supplies and snacks. Find 2 different ways to buy each thing from the school store. Write how many of each coin you need.

Item	Dime	Nickel	Penny	Dime	Nickel	Penny
14¢	4		1	4	2	
6¢						
11¢						
13¢						
18¢						
15¢						

Using Logic

Name ______________________ Date ____________________

Read each problem. Fill in the tables.

Ann, Joe, and Erin work at the school. Ann has students. Joe cleans the school. Erin makes hot lunches. Write each name in the table under the job each one does.

cook	teacher	janitor
Erin	Ann	Joe

1. Pedro, Al, and Cara collect things. Al's collection is sticky. Cara's collection is heavy. Pedro's collection is from the beach. Write each name in the table under the thing each one collects.

stamps	shells	rocks

2. Dino, Will, and Liz play sports. Dino kicks a ball. Will hits a ball. Liz bounces a ball. Write each name in the table under the sport each one plays.

soccer	basketball	baseball

3. Lori, Sai, and Chad had drinks with a snack. Lori's drink was white. Sai's drink had bubbles. Chad's drink was warm. Write each name in the table under the drink each one had.

cocoa	milk	soda

Name ______________________ Date ____________________

Follow the directions to solve each problem.

I. Add. Find the pattern. Write the next problem.

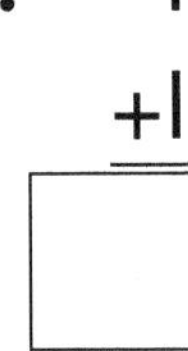

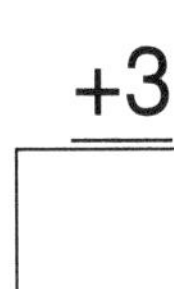

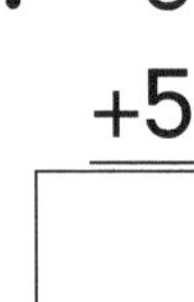

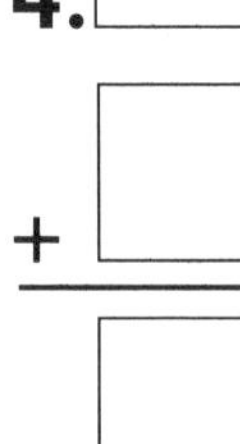

---

5. Make a drawing to solve the problem. There were 10 jars on the shelf. 4 jars fell off the shelf. How many jars were left on the shelf?

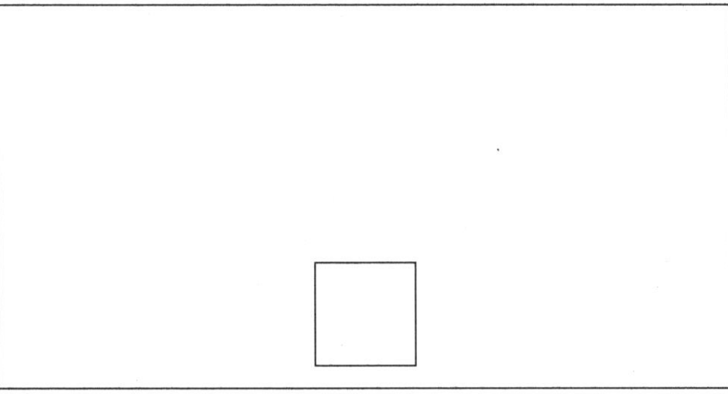

---

6. Write a number sentence to solve the problem. Mike's Bike Shop has 4 blue bikes in the window. There are 6 red bikes in the window. How many bikes are in the window?

☐ ________ ◯ ☐ ________ = ☐ ________

---

7. Read the problem. Fill in the table. Donnie, Melissa, and Jeff ate some fruit. Donnie's fruit was yellow. Melissa's fruit was red. Jeff's fruit was purple. Write each name in the table under the fruit each one ate.

plum	banana	apple

Choosing a Strategy

Name ______________________ Date ____________________

1. Write the number that is next in the pattern. Write the pattern.

2 → 5 → 8 → ____ 6 → 8 → 10 → ____

______________ ______________

2. Find 2 different ways to buy each thing from the bakery. Write how many of each coin you need.

= 10¢ = 5¢ = 1¢

3. Look at each picture. Find the pattern. Circle the shape that is next in the pattern.

    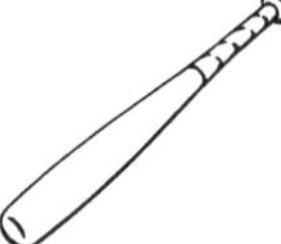 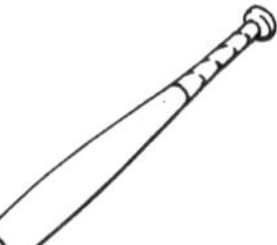 

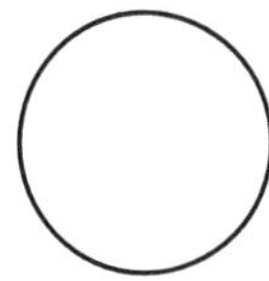 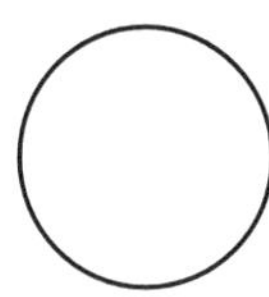  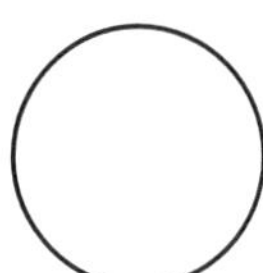 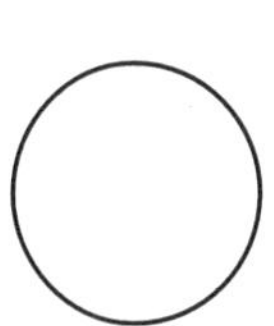 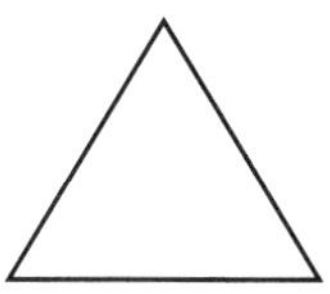

Name ______________________ Date ___________________

Follow the directions to solve each problem. Write the number in the box.

Vic counted his hats and made a graph. The graph shows how many hats he has. Use the graph to solve the problems.

Vic's Hats

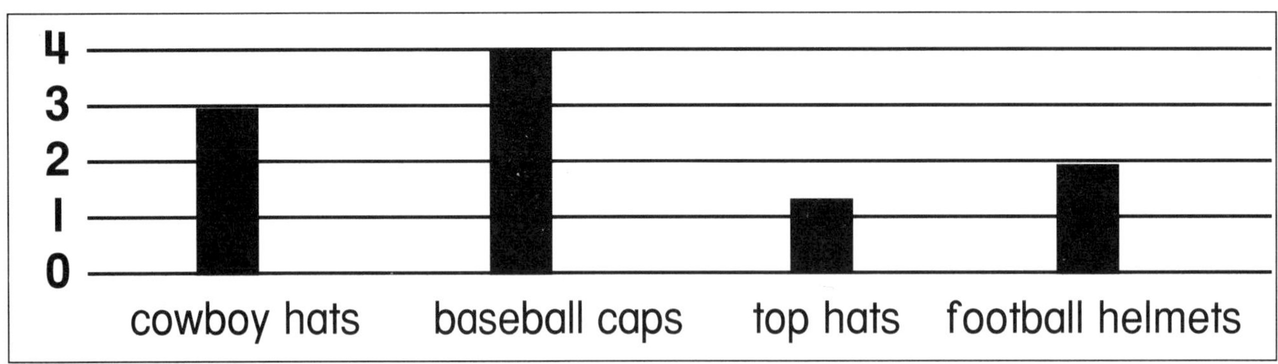

1. How many baseball caps does Vic have? ☐
2. How many more cowboy hats than football helmets does he have? ☐

Sam made 3 kinds of cookies. He sold them at a bake sale and made a graph to see how many he sold.

Cookies Sold

3. How many more sugar cookies than raisin cookies did he sell? ☐
4. How many cookies did Sam sell in all? ☐

Name ____________________ Date ____________________

You need:

- Pictures of a variety of foods (Drawn or cut from magazines)
- Crayons or pencils

1. What are the four main food groups?

2. Draw or paste a picture of a good meal.

   Why is this meal good for you?

3. Name a food that is not good for you. Why is this food not good for you?

Classifying Foods

Name ______________________ Date ____________________

Separating Mixtures

You need:
- Bucket of sand
- Cup of dirt
- 3-4 cups of water
- Cup of water
- Filter and large bowl

1. Pour the water into the bucket of sand. What happens?

Why do you think this happens?

2. Pour the sand and water into the filter. What happens?

Why?

3. Pour the cup of water into the cup of dirt. What happens?

Name ______________________ Date ____________________

Rock Layers

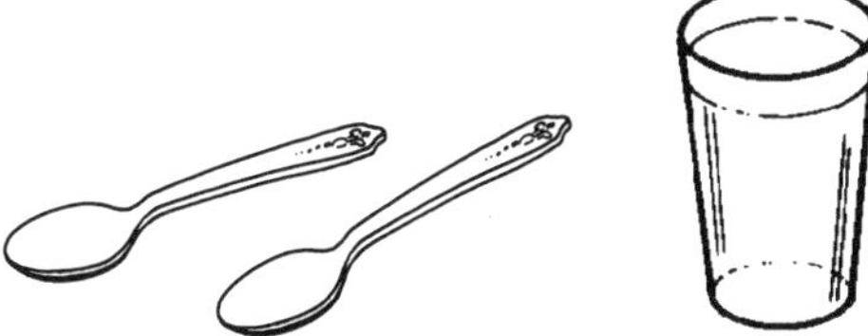

You need:
- Sand
- Flour
- Cocoa
- Sugar
- Clear plastic cup

1. Put 2-3 spoonfuls of sand into the cup.
2. Put 2-3 spoonfuls of flour into the cup. Do not mix.
3. Put 2-3 spoonfuls of cocoa into the cup. Do not mix.
4. Put 2-3 spoonfuls of sugar into the cup. Do not mix.

1. How many layers are in the cup? ____________________
2. Which layer did you put in first? ____________________
3. Which layer is on the bottom of the cup? ____________________
4. How many layers are above the flour? ____________________
5. Which is the oldest layer? ____________________
6. Which is the youngest layer? ____________________
7. How are these layers like layers of Earth? ____________________

Name ____________________ Date ____________________

Seasons

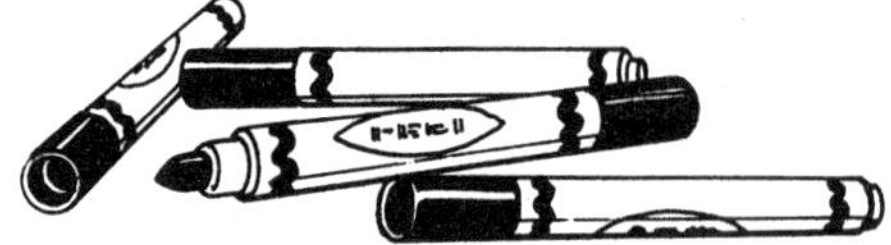

You need:
- Crayons
- Pencils

1. What are the four seasons? ____________________

2. Which season is the coldest? ____________________

3. Which season is after summer? ____________________

4. What season brings May flowers? ____________________

5. What season is it in July? ____________________

Draw a picture of what you might do or wear in the winter.	Draw a picture of what you might do or wear in the spring.	Draw a picture of what you might do and wear in the summer.	Draw a picture of what you might do or wear in the fall.

Ordering Events/Seasons

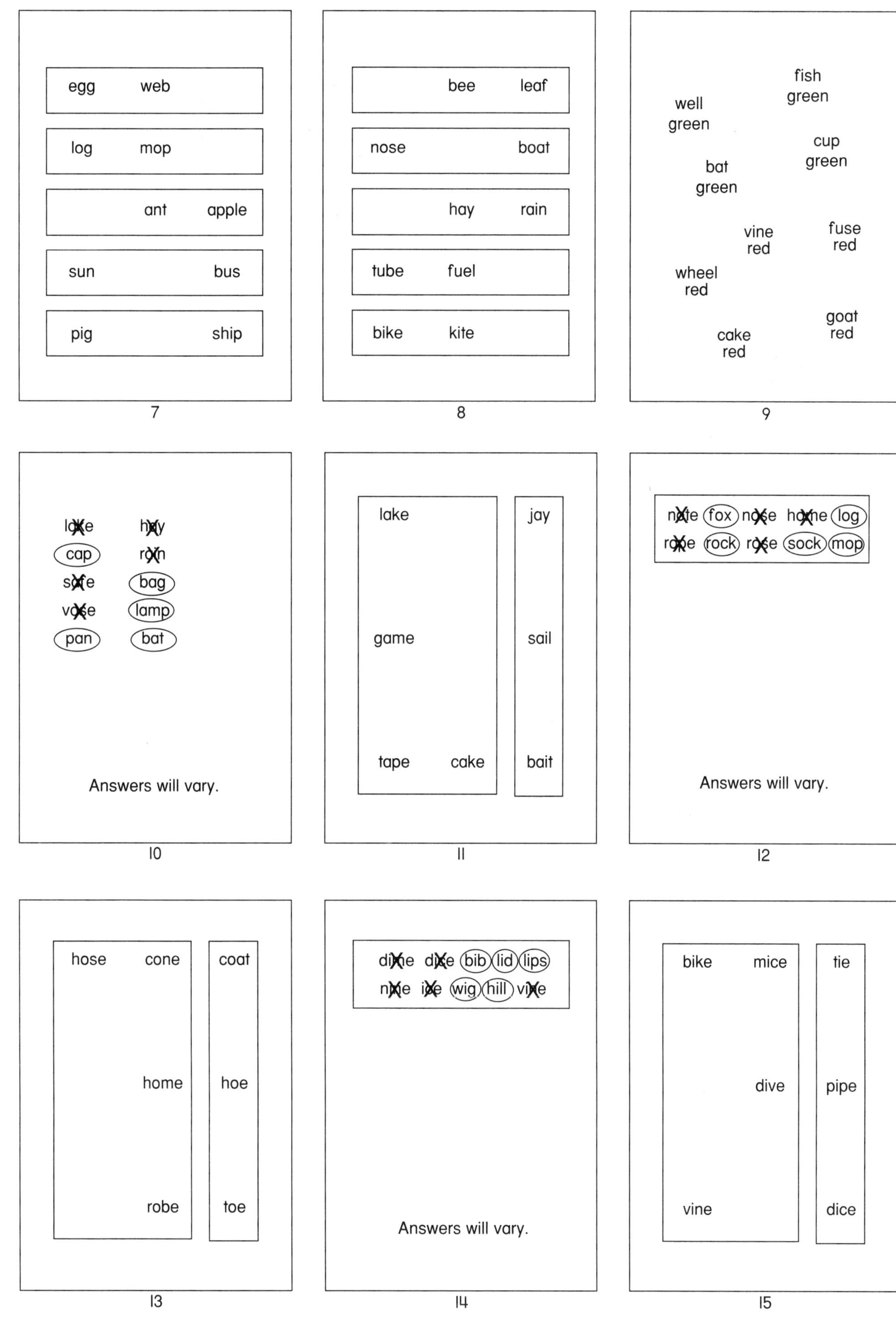

egg web
log mop
ant apple
sun bus
pig ship
7
bee leaf
nose boat
hay rain
tube fuel
bike kite
8
fish green
well green
cup green
bat green
vine red
fuse red
wheel red
goat red
cake red
9
lake hay
cap rain
safe bag
vase lamp
pan bat
Answers will vary.
10
lake jay
game sail
tape cake bait
11
note fox nose home log
rope rock rose sock mop
Answers will vary.
12
hose cone coat
home hoe
robe toe
13
dime dice bib lid lips
nine ice wig hill vine
Answers will vary.
14
bike mice tie
dive pipe
vine dice
15

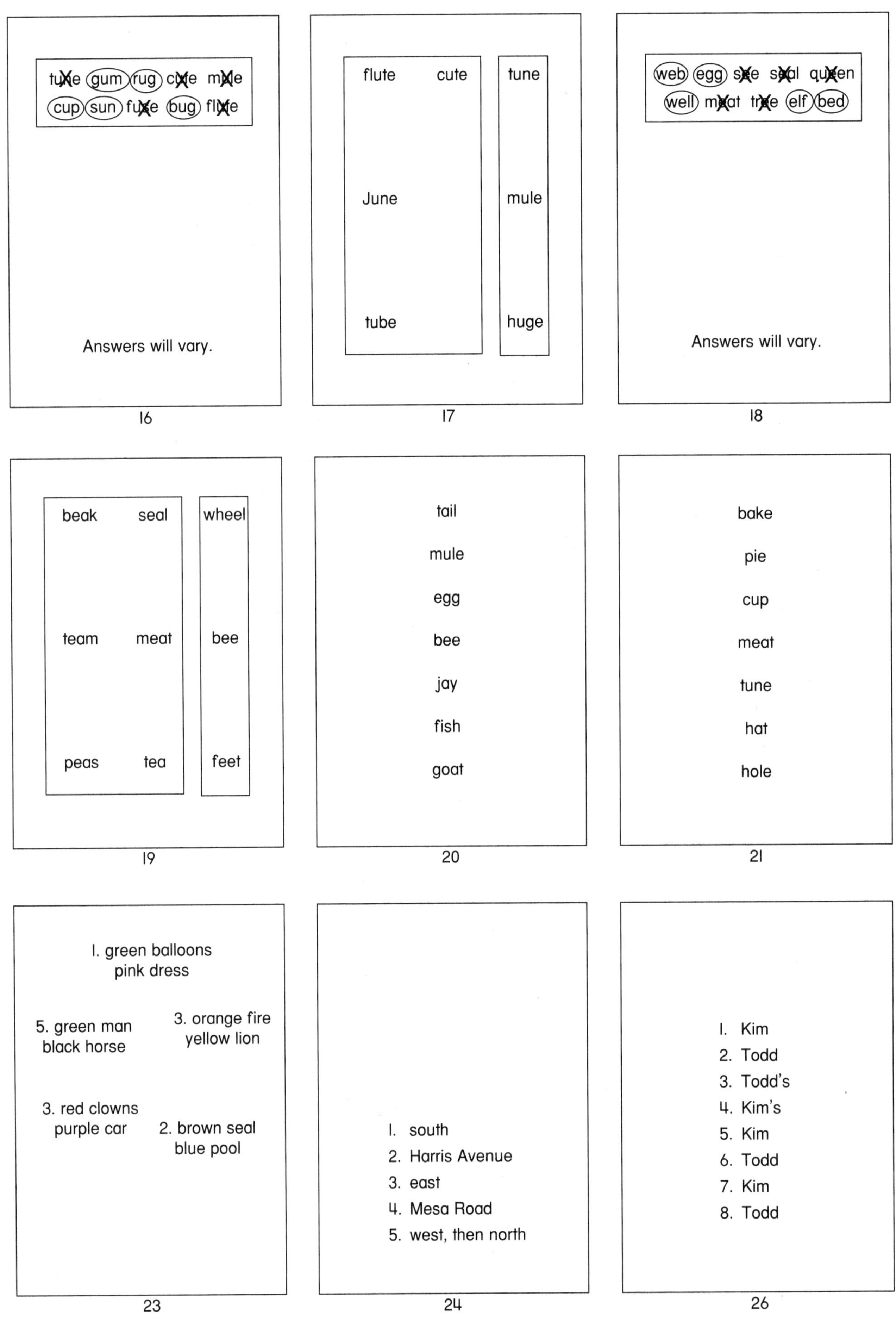

16

tuXe gum rug cuXe muXe
cup sun fuXe bug fluXe

Answers will vary.

17

flute cute tune
June mule
tube huge

18

web egg seXe seXal queXen
well meXat treXe elf bed

Answers will vary.

19

beak seal wheel
team meat bee
peas tea feet

20

tail
mule
egg
bee
jay
fish
goat

21

bake
pie
cup
meat
tune
hat
hole

23

1. green balloons
pink dress

5. green man
black horse

3. orange fire
yellow lion

3. red clowns
purple car

2. brown seal
blue pool

24

1. south
2. Harris Avenue
3. east
4. Mesa Road
5. west, then north

26

1. Kim
2. Todd
3. Todd's
4. Kim's
5. Kim
6. Todd
7. Kim
8. Todd

1. d
2. a
3. c
4. b
5. c
6. d

27

dogs
big
long
two
four
tail

28

2
6
1
4
3
5

29

1. corn
2. parrot
3. car
4. hat
5. pool

30

1. frog
2. apple
3. kitten
4. tree
5. sneakers
6. crayon

31

1. seal
   fish
2. doll
   yo-yo
3. coat
   ring

32

hat	dress
shorts	shoes
happy	no hat
no shoes	sad

33

1. is a big horse
   lives in a barn
   runs in a field
   eats grass
   gives Teri a ride
2. is a brown puppy
   has a black nose
   lives in the house
   sleeps on a mat
   plays with a ball

34

1. Lee's
2. Mia's
3. store
4. Jay

35

I. small hat

2. medium door

3. small shoe

4. large doghouse

36

I. 5 minutes

2. 10 minutes

3. 6 days

4. I hour

37

2 4

I 5 3

38

A. I
3
2

B. 3
2
I

C. 2
I
3

D. 3
2
I

39

T	D
L	Q
F	J
N	W
Q	X
G	J
T	D
L	R
A	F
W	P
T	D
I	K

40

I. run
2. Sally
3. ugly
4. cat
5. fish

6.	7.	8.
angry	cake	dance
sad	sandwich	run
happy	apple	give
confused	cheese	eat

41

I. Sunday
2. Thursday
3. Wednesday
4. Tuesday
5. Answers will vary.

I. Sun.
2. Mon.
3. Tues.
4. Wed.
5. Thurs.
6. Fri.
7. Sat.

42

I.	January	Jan.
2.	February	Feb.
3.	March	Mar.
4.	April	Apr.
5.	May	May
6.	June	June
7.	July	July
8.	August	Aug.
9.	September	Sept.
10.	October	Oct.
II.	November	Nov.
12.	December	Dec.

43

I. summer
2. fall
3. winter
4. spring

Answers will vary.

44

1. Samir reads books.
2. My sister drinks juice.
3. Chang caught a ball.
4. I go to the library.
5. We play at the park.
6. Ray has a dog.
7. José paints a picture.

45

1. Sue loves her puppy.
2. His name is Shag.
3. Furry X dogs.
4. Sue plays with Shag.
5. Chases X a ball.
6. Do you like dogs?
7. Where is Sue?
8. Why X did?
9. Dogs and X cats?
10. Can you see Shag?

46

1. Inez
2. Pedro
3. Manny and Rosa
4. My family and I
5. shops
6. cooks
7. wash
8. work

47

1. A
2. T
3. A
4. T
5. A
6. My friend - blue
   goes - red
7. Monkeys - blue
   climb - red
8. Tigers - blue
   roar - red
9. Whales - blue
   swim - red
10. The giraffe - blue
    eats - red

48

1. tree
2. pit
3. goat
4. rug
5. cap
6. bike
7. box
8. bed
9. lake

49

1. crawl
2. juice
3. book
4. break
5. wear
6. pour
7. dirt

50

1. The Flat Tire
2. Kinds of Twins
3. The Race

51

1. We had fun on our shopping trip.
2. Mariko was getting ready for bed.
3. This is how a rainbow forms.
4. Gordon planted a garden.

52

1. Eric is an artist.
2. I read a good story today.
3. I like to visit Grandma.

53

1. a fish

2. ice cream

3. a clock

4. Market St.

54

1. Mandy's house

2. Mandy

3. got bread

4. Working Together

55

1. Jill

2. Leon

3. last week

4. The Big Race

5. Answers will vary.

56

1. a parade

2. a marching band

3. Fourth of July

4. Fourth of July Celebration

5. Answers will vary.

57

1. Saturday morning

2. They had to stay inside.

3. The Rainy Day

4. Answers will vary.

58

1. grow

2. home

59

1. team

2. plays

3. winners

4. alone

60

1. clock

2. heat

3. Art

61

1. song

2. map

3. zoo

62

1. larger
2. friends
3. swim

63

1. move
2. smart
3. taste

64

1. happy
2. books
3. boats

65

1. ears
2. ready
3. leave

66

1. mittens
2. clouds
3. job

67

1. music
2. store
3. cats

68

1. sky
2. near
3. small

69

1. heavy
2. herd
3. friendly

70

1. land
2. food
3. extinct

71

1. tools

2. fun

3. places

72

1. trash

2. good

3. age

73

11	13
15	17
14	18

74

12

11

11	12	12	11
12	12	11	11
2	7	11	3

9 + 3 = 12

75

14

13

14	13	13	14
14	14	13	14
4	0	4	13

76

16

15

15	16	15	15
15	16	16	15
3	3	10	2

5 + 11 = 16

77

17

18

17	17	18	18
17	17	18	18
10	4	18	13

13 + 5 = 18

78

19

19

17	18	19	16
11	19	17	18
14	5	5	4

3 + 16 = 19

79

19	12	8	18
18	13	19	13
14	12	9	19
14	15	18	11
9	15	16	17

80

11 19 18 17

17 14 13 13

12 18 15 14

16 17 19 10

16 10 19 13

81

19 19 18 15

9 10 19 10

14 16 18 8

4 8 6 7

14 + 5 = 19

82

3 6 2 5

2 0 1 8

2 4 1 2

7 6 4 2

6 – 4 = 2

83

5

7

9

3 11 3 2

7 6 9 5

12 11 8 4

84

5

7

9 4 2 1

10 7 10 4

14 14 2 6

13 – 5 = 8

85

3

7

9 7 1 4

8 11 13 15

16 15 7 16

15 – 6 = 9

86

3

5

11 9 7 5

15 14 1 9

18 17 11 14

18 – 8 = 10

87

8

13

2 5 13 8

5 9 6 11

19 19 17 10

19 – 13 = 6

88

16 7 7 9

3 3 6 9

3 3 4 6

1 2 3 4

8 2 5 7

89

11	2	8	12
2	2	10	4
14	1	7	6
7	8	1	4
6	3	6	17

90

17	12	14	10
2	15	10	9
4	0	7	16
19	6	16	15
			11
		8	

91

1	14	6	12
3	7	19	19
17	9	17	18
3	17	3	7

12 – 2 = 10 – 3 = 7

11 + 6 = 17 – 1 = 16

92

9¢ 12¢

15¢ 16¢

1¢ 19¢ 4¢ 17¢

18¢ – 9¢ = 9¢ – 3¢ = 6¢

13¢ + 5¢ = 18¢

one dime, three pennies
and one nickel

93

3 + 4 = 7

4¢ + 2¢ + 5¢ = 11¢

10 + 9 = 19

12 + 7 = 19

6 + 4 = 10 + 8 = 18

7 + 2 = 9

94

17 – 9 = 8

10 – 6 = 4

14 – 12 = 2

19 – 13 = 6

16 – 11 = 5

15¢ – 10¢ = 5¢

95

4 + 3 = 7

12 – 8 = 4

5 + 4 = 9

17 – 14 = 3

19¢ – 13¢ = 6¢

8 + 3 = 11 + 5 = 16

96

2 + 4 = 6

6 + 7 = 13

7 – 4 = 3

18 – 14 = 4

3 + 5 = 8 + 7 = 15

6 – 3 = 3

97

2 4 8 $\begin{array}{r} 8 \\ +8 \\ \hline 16 \end{array}$

2 3 4 $\begin{array}{r} 10 \\ -5 \\ \hline 5 \end{array}$

3
subtract 3

9
add 2

15
add 5

4
subtract 4

98

6
10 10 10 $\underline{+4}$
10

5
9 7 5 $\underline{-2}$
3

star

circle

right arrow

99

9

13

3

18

100

6

6

16

5

101

2

5

9

12

18

102

5

1

tulips

lilies

12

103

16 ham – 13 turkey = 3 more ham

4 cookies + 5 cookies = 9 cookies in all

19 sodas – 13 sodas = 6 sodas left

12 sack + 5 hot = 17 lunches in all

104

14 birds – 8 birds = 6 birds left

2 rabbits + 7 bunnies = 9 rabbits in all

3 white + 6 brown + 9 mice in all

18 gold – 13 angel = 5 more gold

105

D	N	P	D	N	P
1		4		2	4
	1	1			6
1		1		2	1
1		3		2	3
1	1	3		3	3
1	1			3	

answers may vary

106

Al Pedro Cara

Dino Liz Will

Chad Lori Sai

107

7

2 6 10 $+7$

14

6

4 blue + 6 red = 10 bikes

Jeff Donnie Melissa

108

11 12

add 3 add 2

D	N	P	D	N	P
1	1			3	
	1	2			7

bat

circle

answers may vary

109

4

1

4

15

110

1. grains, cereals; fruits, vegetables; meats; dairy
2. Answers will vary.
3. Answers will vary.

111

1. Answers will vary.
2. Answers will vary.
3. Answers will vary.

112

1. 4
2. sand
3. sand
4. 2
5. sand
6. sugar
7. Answers will vary.

113

1. winter, spring, summer, fall
2. winter
3. fall
4. spring
5. summer

Answers will vary.

114

Name ____________________ Date ____________________

Assessment

Circle the pictures that have **short vowel** sounds.
Put an X on the pictures that have **long vowel** sounds.

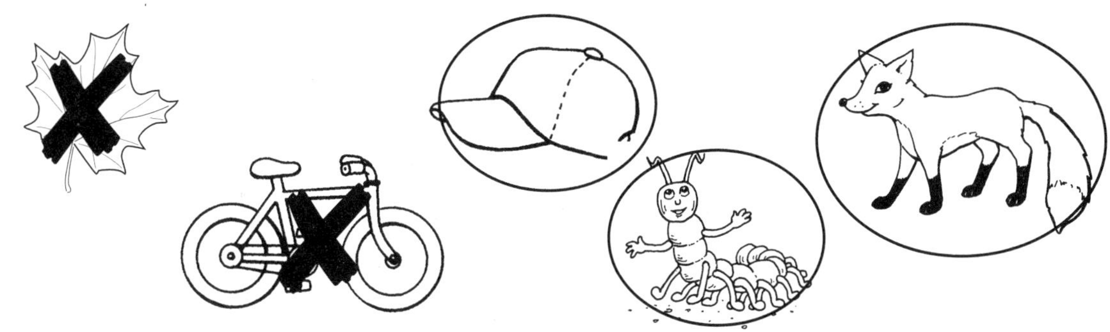

Write the letter of the picture that is different in each row.

a **b** **c** **d**

d

a **b** **c** **d**

c

Circle the naming part of each sentence in blue.
Circle the action part of each sentence in red.

1. My friend goes to the zoo with me.
2. Monkeys climb trees.
3. Tigers roar loudly.

Assessment Answer Key

Name ______________________ Date ______________________

Assessment

Write the number in the box.

1. 16 + 3 = 19

2. 17 − 2 = 15

3. 13 − 5 = 8

4. 9 + 7 = 16

5. Jodi's cat had 5 kittens. Sari's cat had 6 kittens. How many kittens did the girls have in all?

11

6. Write the next number in the pattern. 2 → 4 → 7 → 11 → 16

7. Find 2 different ways to buy the cookie. Write how many of each coin you need.

1 2

7

8. Name four main food groups.

cereals, grains **meats** **dairy** **fruits, vegetables**

9. When you pour water and sand into a filter, what happens to the sand? **The sand stays in the filter.**

10. Name the four seasons.

winter **spring** **summer** **fall**